Using picture books

by Hilary White

Contents

Using picture books to support the six areas of learning:

Published by Step Forward Publishing Limited
The Coach House, Cross Road, Leamington Spa CV32 5PB   Tel: 01926 420046
© Step Forward Publishing Limited 2001
Using Picture Books   ISBN: 1-902438-44-2

About this book

This book takes a close look at the world of picture books and how they can help the young child's development and learning.

The first section explores the special role of picture books in the following areas of learning:

◆ Personal, Social and Emotional Development
◆ Communication, Language and Literacy
◆ Mathematical Development
◆ Knowledge and Understanding of the World
◆ Physical Development
◆ Creative Development

It includes suggestions for ways of using picture books and gives lots of examples, both to illustrate and explain points and as recommendations for sharing with your children. Wherever possible, well-known and popular books have been chosen. At the time of publication, all of the recommended books were still in print. Occasionally, however, even a classic title goes out of print. If this becomes the case, it is worth checking whether a large bookshop chain has a copy left on its shelves. Alternatively, you can order from your local library, which should be willing to borrow from outside the region if it does not hold a copy of the book you want.

THE PICTURE BOOKS
The next section concentrates on 12 classic and well-known picture books (listed right), many of which will be familiar to you.

Each book has its own section, which follows a set format:

◆ a short introduction to the book, explaining the story and how the book works
◆ at least three planned activities linked to the themes of the book
◆ two or three short activities

The 12 books cover a range of target age groups. For example, *Dear Zoo* and *The Very Hungry Caterpillar* are perfect for your youngest children whereas *Who's Who in Our Street?* and *Dear Daddy* will stretch your oldest. This does not mean that you cannot use the books with the entire Foundation Stage age range. There is a lot for even the youngest children to explore in the pictures of *Dear Daddy* while older ones will enjoy revisiting *Dear Zoo* and can gain a great deal from the associated activities.

THE ACTIVITIES
The main activities can be adapted to suit your age group, your setting and to fit the time you have available. The 'five-minute activities' can be slipped into the odd few minutes at the end of a session or done on the spur of the moment. The activities cover all areas of learning and a wide range of themes, topics and knowledge areas, including shape, size, colour, number, opposites and contrasts, seasons, weather, time, night and day, weekdays, animals, homes, buildings and food. They include sorting, matching, counting, role play, art and craft, music, experiments, discussion and other typical pre-school activities.

A list of themes and activities is given for each book on pages 86-87. This provides an overview of what the books and activities have to offer and can be used to help with planning and preparation.

Few picture books have numbered pages, so where an activity links with a particular page or picture in the book, that page is identified as an 'opening', followed by a number (opening 3, opening 5). Count the front cover as opening 1 and then simply progress from there. In a number of books you will be at opening 3 or 4 before the story actually begins.

Wherever possible, encourage the children to develop the activities in

The 12 books

Grandpa's Handkerchief by Dorothy Clark Illustrated by Siobhan Dodds
Publisher: Hodder Children's Books ISBN: 0 7500 0784 2

Dear Zoo by Rod Campbell
Publisher: Puffin
ISBN: 0 14 050446 X

Mr Gumpy's Outing by John Burningham
Publisher: Puffin
ISBN: 0 14 050254 8

The Blue Balloon by Mick Inkpen
Publisher: Hodder Children's Books ISBN: 0 340 75738 8

Washing Line by Jez Alborough
Publisher: Walker
ISBN: 0 7445 6309 7

The Very Hungry Caterpillar by Eric Carle
Publisher: Puffin
ISBN: 0 14 050087 1

Rosie's Walk by Pat Hutchins
Publisher: Puffin
ISBN: 0 14 050032 4

Ten, Nine, Eight by Molly Bang
Publisher: Red Fox
ISBN: 0 09 935441 1

The Nursery Collection by Shirley Hughes
Publisher: Walker
ISBN: 0 7445 4378 9

Dear Daddy by Philippe Dupasquier
Publisher: Puffin
ISBN: 0 14 050540 7

Who's Who in Our Street? by Jan Ormerod
Publisher: Red Fox
ISBN: 0 09 926289 4

Farmer Duck by Martin Waddell Illustrated by Helen Oxenbury
Publisher: Walker
ISBN: 0 7445 3660 X

(Publishers and ISBNs listed are all for paperback editions.)

their own way. For example, the art and craft activities give specific suggestions for materials and techniques. These can be used as pointers, but ideally the children should be able to choose their own techniques and materials - particularly older ones. A number of activities also require the child to talk about a topic or picture so that the adult can record what the child has to say in writing. As much as possible, do this in front of the child to help her discover the purpose and process of writing. Encourage older children to use emergent writing to write their own pieces.

A number of activities are interchangeable from one book to another. For example, 'Making a number sequence' can be linked with *The Very Hungry Caterpillar, Washing Line, Mr Gumpy's Outing* or *Ten, Nine, Eight*. In the most obvious cases, a note has been added to suggest ways of adapting an activity so that it can be linked with a different book.

FOLLOW-UP LEARNING

A number of activities give suggestions for setting out materials, equipment or role-play props so that the children can continue to explore an activity through free play. This independent exploration is an important aspect of the learning process. Suggestions are also given for setting up displays linked to the activity or showing the children's work. Think through how to design the display so that it will attract the children and provide further learning opportunities. Encourage the children to help with planning and organising the display and refer to it as much as possible.

ASSESSMENT AND EARLY LEARNING GOALS

Each activity has a list of relevant Early Learning Goals. The lists are fairly comprehensive but do not necessarily include every single goal met by the activity. Most activities satisfy a number

of the Personal, Social and Emotional and Communication, Language and Literacy goals. For example, any activity that grasps the child's interest will satisfy the goal: 'continue to be interested, excited and motivated to learn'; any activity that involves talk and explanation will satisfy 'interact with others, negotiating plans and taking turns in conversation'. Those included in the lists are the most significant and obvious goals for each activity.

Each activity also includes an assessment section in the form of questions to answer and signs to look out for.

What is a picture book?

Picture books come in all shapes and sizes - from the tiny board book designed to fit snugly into a toddler's hand to the big poster-sized books for use with a large group of children. Many picture books nowadays offer much more than a cover and a few pages. New technology has enabled publishers to create books that light up, play music and produce any number of sound effects. A picture book no longer has to be book-shaped, either. Some come in the form of jigsaw puzzles and games, or in the shape of a sandwich or a vehicle with wheels. Open up the pages and out pops a series of three-dimensional paper sculptures. Some pages have tabs to be pulled and flaps to peep behind. Some are made up of different textures so that the pictures can be stroked and rubbed, as well as looked at.

All this variety and inventiveness makes it difficult to say exactly what a picture book is. In the end, any book with pictures counts as a picture book, as long as the pictures are at least as important as the words in telling the story or presenting the theme. The illustrated story aimed at the older child is not really a picture book because the story would not change or suffer if the illustrations were removed. A few picture books have no words at all, either because the book is aimed at very young babies or because the picture book maker has decided to tell a story in pictures only. Raymond Briggs' *The Snowman* (Puffin) is a well-known example of a story which has no text.

Most picture books are designed for the pre-school and Key Stage 1 age

group, ranging from the baby to the six-year-old. A few explore themes that are not suitable for the pre-school age group. Although Raymond Briggs' *The Snowman* is delightful for little ones, many of his books are more appropriate for the older junior age range, as are the picture books of Anthony Browne.

As well as coming in a huge variety of forms and packages, picture books also cover just about any topic or theme imaginable. Nursery rhymes, poetry and song collections, rhyming texts, imaginative re-tellings of fairy stories, everyday and fantasy stories, information and concept books, puzzle books, stories to help children cope with life events, alphabet books, number books .... the list is endless.

Four babies in buggies,

From: *The Nursery Collection*

WHY PICTURE BOOKS?

SOMETHING FOR EVERY OCCASION
Picture books are affordable, accessible, fun and versatile. A picture book makes a good springboard for

discussion or the starting point for extended topic work. The story and pictures can help the child make sense of what she has already experienced as well as learn about new people, places and things. Alternatively, a book is perfect for filling those few minutes at the end of a session or as a focus for children who are finding it difficult to settle. You can share a picture book with the whole group or you can encourage the children to look at the words and pictures by themselves. A carefully chosen book can also be used as a valuable link between you and a child with special needs or a child who does not have English as a first language.

ARE YOU SITTING QUIETLY?
While we no longer expect young children to remain glued to their seats, it is still important that they learn to sit quietly and listen. This is much easier for the child if she is interested - and a good book is one of the quickest ways of catching and holding the child's attention. The best writers and illustrators are extremely skilful at creating stories and pictures to fascinate young children. Using a picture book as a focus gives you a head start when it comes to helping the child settle within a group. Hold as many story groups as you can and encourage families to read at home, to help the child develop his or her concentration.

JOINING IN THE STORY
Of course, story time should not only be about sitting still and listening. Books can provide lots of opportunity to engage in active learning through discussion, joining in the last words of a repetitive text, role play or acting out little parts in the story. Although we tend to think of story time as a passive activity, the child is actually very busy in her mind making sense of the story. The more we can follow up questions,

comments and story-based discussion, the richer the child's experience will be.

REPETITION: THE SAME EACH TIME

One of the most useful aspects of a book is that you can read it again and again and again. Repetition is important for the young child's learning - from the daily routine of bedtime to repeated alphabet songs and counting rhymes. The picture book provides a particularly good form of repetition. Unlike real life events, which are bound to vary from day to day, the story and pictures in the book remain exactly the same with each reading. This gives a clear-cut opportunity for understanding to develop. If you re-read the same book to a small group, look out for how the questions and comments build on the discussion that took place the last time you shared the book. Look for signs that the child's knowledge and understanding is growing with each reading. Another useful aspect is that the picture remains constant. You and the children can look at it and talk about it for as long as you want to without anything moving or changing. And the picture will be exactly the same when you go back to the book the next day.

BOOKS OR VIDEOS?

Of course, children have lots of other experiences that appear similar to books. Video tapes are often compared to picture books. Both tell a story; both use words and pictures; both encourage children to sit, look and listen. Videos certainly have their uses, but they will never be able to provide a complete substitute for books. During story time, it is easy to stop, chat and look at the picture for as long as you want to. You can skip back a few pages to check something or re-read a page. Because you are reading the book to the child, you are central to the whole process. You can answer questions, engage in discussion, monitor levels of concentration and adjust your reading accordingly. Your involvement makes the whole story experience doubly useful and enjoyable for the child. Imagine all the rewinding and fast-forwarding if you tried to do the same

with a video! Unlike picture book sharing, the video is not a sociable experience for the young child who learns so much from sharing her thoughts and ideas with adults and other children.

"How goes the work?"
"Quack!"

"How goes the work?"
"Quack!"

From: Farmer Duck

child whose attention is wandering, try drawing her back into the story by using her name: 'And what do you think happened next, Shauna? The cat jumped over the hedge.'

READING ALOUD - SOME PRACTICAL TIPS

The beauty of a book is that it provides everything you need in one small package: a story to listen to, colourful detailed pictures to look at, the familiar and comforting, the exciting and the new. Anyone can sit down and share a book with a child - which is useful if you have parent helpers or students coming into your setting. Having said that, there are certain skills you can develop, to increase your ability to capture the child's attention and make the most of the story.

◆ Unless you are a confident and experienced reader, get to know the book thoroughly before you share it with the children. It is not easy to keep an eye on your group if you have to concentrate too much on the words themselves.

◆ Make eye contact with the children as much as possible. If you spot a

◆ Make the most of the pictures. Try to ensure that the children can see the pictures all the time. Work on your ability to read upside down or sideways so that you can hold the book open on your lap or up to one side. The picture can provide you with another means of drawing the child back into the story. Point to and talk about interesting details or ask a question such as: 'Tom, can you see the mouse hiding from the cat?'

◆ Keep story sessions short while your group are still learning to sit and listen to a story. If the group loses concentration, wind up the session swiftly by paraphrasing the story. This is much easier to do if you know the story well.

◆ Try always to finish off the story, even when the group is restless. Children need to realise that a story has an ending so that they will stay listening to find out what happens in the end. If stories often remain unfinished, it will take the child much longer to discover the pleasures of 'the ending'.

◆ With new or younger children, keep your voice as even and normal as possible. It can be a bit disturbing if you suddenly change character, particularly if you are able to turn in a convincing performance.

◆ As your children become more used to you and the setting, you can vary your voice to fit the mood of the story. Introduce different voices for different characters. Use pauses to build up excitement and have fun with different facial expressions.

◆ How you organise your group will depend on its size, the purpose you have in mind and the possibilities available to you in your setting. When you want story time to be relaxing, choose an informal arrangement of children gathered around your knee. With two or three children, you can arrange them so that they are either side of you, looking at the pictures and print as you read.

◆ If you need to use a more formal arrangement, either for a large group or to minimise distractions, try a semi-circle of chairs. This is the most effective arrangement for showing the pictures to all the children in the group.

WHAT TO CHOOSE?
There is a huge range of good books to choose from nowadays, and lots of

From: *Mr Gumpy's Outing*

information available in the library, bookshop or on the Internet. Ask your children's librarian for suggestions over what to choose, particularly if you have a topic in mind. All the major children's publishers run advisory services for schools. Send away for copies of their catalogues, listing their collection of books. Most of the catalogues include a short review of each book and a recommended age range. Look out for *The Picture Book Index* (compiled by Margaret Smyth and published by the Association of Assistant Librarians) in the reference section of your library. This useful book lists a wide range of well-known picture books, divided up into just about every theme you can think of.

Choosing the appropriate age range for a book can be difficult as children vary so much in what they are ready for. Treat any age recommendation as no more than a guideline and go with your own instincts and knowledge of the children in the group. Many picture books can be enjoyed on different levels. Your choice will also depend on whether you are choosing

a book for an individual, a small group or a large group.

A large group in the early years setting will usually include a mixture of ages and developmental levels. Where this is the case, aim your choice at the younger ones. Older children will usually enjoy a book for little ones, particularly a clever and multi-layered story such as Rod Campbell's *Dear Zoo* or Pat Hutchins' *Rosie's Walk*. If a number of your story sessions take place with a larger, mixed age group, do make sure that older children are given plenty of books chosen specifically for their interest and ability level.

With large groups, try to use books in the biggest format you can find. If you can borrow or invest in some big books, these are ideal. If some pictures are too small to be seen easily, walk around the group so that each child can have a closer look. Always try to put the book you have read in the book corner so that the child can choose to look at it again by herself.

Personal, Social and Emotional Development

The child's personal, social and emotional development provides the foundation for success in all other aspects of her life. It covers a wide range of skills and capabilities, including the ability to work harmoniously with others, the development of respect for people from other cultures and an awareness of right and wrong.

WORKING IN HARMONY WITH OTHERS

The group activity of story time offers some unique opportunities to co-exist harmoniously with others. In the first instance, the children must learn to sit quietly and not speak while the story is being read. They have to organise themselves so that nobody prevents anyone else from seeing the pictures - particularly where you have a group sitting around your feet on the carpet. The disturbing effects of somebody talking or blocking your view are immediately obvious to the children because the thread of the story is broken. This in turn helps children to learn that self-control is important in order not to spoil the experience for others. The more often you hold story groups, the more opportunities the children have to develop the ability to co-operate within a group and show awareness of other people's needs.

It is also useful to establish some rules regarding interruptions. On the one hand, story based conversation is valuable. On the other hand, even valid and interesting interruptions will break a child's concentration, particularly in a large group. One way around this is to hold small group story sessions where conversation is encouraged. You can then limit interruptions in a large group, where it is harder to ensure that all the children have picked up the threads of the story again once the interruption is over. Whatever rules you decide on, the children will gain a valuable lesson in group co-operation through learning to follow them.

DIFFERENT CULTURES

There is now a huge range of excellent choices available to enable children to discover the differences and similarities between people from other cultures, races and backgrounds.

When choosing for the pre-school age group, look out for elements that the child can identify with as well as the clear and thoughtful presentation of cultural differences. Prodeepta Das's beautifully photographed *Geeta's Day* (Frances Lincoln) shows a day in the life of a little girl who lives in an Indian village. Everything is so different from this country and yet the children play, swim, go to school and eat their evening meal with their family. Geeta herself peers out from the pictures with a broad smile, welcoming the reader into her world. She may live a different life from British children, but she has a universal appeal that even little ones will be able to connect with.

Other good examples include Trish Cooke and Helen Oxenbury's *So Much* (Walker), a story set in an Afro-Caribbean home; Kim Lewis's *Floss* or *Emma's Lamb* (Walker), set in an English farm; Mairi Hedderwick's *Katie Morag* stories (Random House), set on the Scottish island of Struay and Shirley Hughes' *Lucy and Tom* stories (Puffin) and *Alfie* stories (Red Fox), which are firmly rooted in an English, mixed race, urban setting. Look at each book from the viewpoint of your children. For a group of children who live in the middle of the English countryside, Shirley Hughes offers a different world. For children from an inner city environment, *So Much* may be familiar and recognisable whereas the setting of Kim Lewis's farming stories could seem almost as foreign as Geeta's Indian village. Have a variety of books in your setting so that you are both reflecting the children's home life and introducing new and different life styles.

DIFFERENT BELIEFS

Festivals and celebrations are a significant aspect of different cultures. The colours, sights, sounds, smells and tastes of festivals such as Diwali, Christmas, the Chinese New Year and Caribbean Carnival make a strong impact on young children and demonstrate the pleasures to be gained from exploring other cultures. Books provide the next best thing to celebrating the festival itself. A book also has the capacity to bring together a number of different elements so that the child gets a comprehensive but manageable introduction to the festival as a whole.

It is not always easy to find information books suitable for the pre-school age range, particularly where multicultural issues are concerned. Wayland publishes a series called *Celebrate!* with separate titles for Chinese New Year, Diwali, Christmas and Id-Ul-Fitr. Although the text is aimed at Key Stage 2 (seven plus), the colour photographs are suitable for any age group. A child's information book can also make a quick, accessible reference for you, particularly in a field with which you are unfamiliar. Study the text carefully and adapt its contents to a level suitable for your particular group.

Better still for this age group are books that disseminate information about other cultures and beliefs through story. Errol Lloyd's *Nini at Carnival* (Red Fox) is a brightly illustrated picture book based on a child attending a Caribbean carnival. Stories about Christmas are also easy to find.

Personal, Social and Emotional Development

One of the best is Brian Wildsmith's *Christmas Story* (Oxford University Press), sumptuously illustrated with glowing jewel-like colours and gold backgrounds. For older children, Nicholas Allen's *Jesus' Christmas Party* (Red Fox) is unbeatable when it comes to combining the essence of the Christmas message with heartwarming good humour.

TRADITIONAL TALES AND RHYMES

Folk tales and rhymes can make an enticing introduction to other cultures for young children. The language, rhythms, characters and settings of traditional stories are good at evoking the flavour of different cultures. If

This means that you have to take a twofold look at any traditional story, particularly if you have a mixed race group: does it reflect a child's home culture or does it introduce the traditions of a new culture? And where do home culture and other cultures start to blend? Many fairy stories we would regard as English had their origins in Eastern European, French or German folk tales. Children growing up in multiracial communities will be aware of both Diwali and Christmas, Caribbean Carnival and Bonfire Night. If you are truly going to reflect and enlighten your group's cultural development through picture books, you will need to give some careful thought to what you should include in your book corner.

author/illustrator and his *Granpa* (Puffin) is a wonderful tribute to the friendship that can exist between grandparents and their grandchildren. However, I feel an entirely personal discomfort with its final picture, where the grandchild is shown as literally faded and washed out after grandpa's death. Sue Limb's *Come Back Grandma* (Red Fox) may not be quite as creative or unusual as *Granpa*, but I prefer its message that the deceased live on in their children and grandchildren (a sophisticated concept, best saved for older ones).

Another example of a book that needs careful consideration is Satoshi Kitamura and Hiawyn Oram's *Angry Arthur* (Red Fox). In this story, Arthur

From: *Rosie's Walk*

possible, invite people into your setting to pass on traditional stories and rhymes to your children. Failing that, look out for a good book. Fiona Walters and Lisa Berkshire have compiled and illustrated an anthology of traditional tales from across the world, called *Fairy Tales from Far and Wide* (Barefoot Books). For rhymes and jingles, try *Down by the River*, a collection of Caribbean songs collected by Grace Hallworth (Mammoth), or *A Child's Treasury of Irish Rhymes* compiled by Alice Taylor (Barefoot Books.)

As well as folk traditions from other cultures, the child needs to learn about those of her own home culture.

LIFE CHALLENGES AND MORAL ISSUES

One of the most useful things about a carefully crafted picture book is its ability to deal with sensitive issues in a subtle way. Good writers and illustrators can be remarkably clever at hitting just the right spot and this is invaluable where Personal, Social and Emotional Development is concerned.

You do have to choose carefully, however. Some books that set out to deal with moral issues and life challenges can be a little stilted or, worse still, 'preachy'. Others may contain elements that do not sit comfortably with your own views and feelings. John Burningham is a superb

has a tantrum so big that he splits the world in two and ends up marooned, all by himself in space. One of the distressing things about tantrums for little ones is the sheer power of their own, unleashed emotions. It can be impossible to predict how young children will interpret stories and what they take on board as 'real'. A story that looks at anger in this way is perhaps best saved for older ones, who can step back and enjoy the story as no more than a humorous fantasy.

In the end, with this area of learning more than any other, it is important to go for books that you like and feel comfortable with. Keep an eye out for stories that deal with a variety of life problems so that you always have something up your sleeve to suggest to a parent or use yourself. Sometimes, the best approach for a child in difficulties is to settle down for a quiet few minutes with a carefully chosen book. If you have a child with a worrying event coming up, it is worth checking Jean and Gareth Anderson's *Topsy and Tim* stories (Ladybird). This series covers just about every possibility, from making new friends to visiting the doctor. Topsy and Tim have been around for years, but the books have been updated for children of today. While they may not display the story telling and artistic genius of a Shirley Hughes or a Martin Waddell, they are clear, simple and can be useful when it comes to showing children that they are not alone in the difficulties they face.

Books that deal with delicate issues such as death, or specialised experiences such as going into hospital are often best saved for individual children going through such experiences. There are, however, a number of books that encompass more everyday life events and difficulties. These stories can be safely used with all children, regardless of whether or not they might feel a personal involvement with a problem. Shirley Hughes is good at writing gentle little stories that show how difficulties can be resolved and problems managed. *Alfie Gets in First* deals reassuringly with the horrors of getting accidentally locked into the house by yourself; *Dogger* is about the loss of a comforter and *The Trouble with Jack* focuses on the perennial problem of having a younger sibling (all published by Red Fox). From the other side of the fence, Pat Hutchins' *Titch* stories (Red Fox) look sensitively at how to cope with being the youngest in the family while Martin Waddell's classic *Can't You Sleep Little Bear?* (Walker) is all about night-time fears. Jill Murphy's *The Last Noo Noo* is a hilarious treat for all children, whether they are trying to give up a dummy or not, while her *Five Minutes Peace* gives children the rare opportunity to look at life from Mum's point of view (both published by Walker).

Many picture books also contain more general, underlying moral messages that can be talked about and role played as part of your work in Personal, Social and Emotional Development. David McKee is one of those author/artists who successfully handles broad moral issues through warmth and humour. *Elmer* takes a highly original yet thoughtful look at being different while *Tusk, Tusk* bravely (and sensitively) deals with racial intolerance

(both Red Fox). Martin Waddell and Helen Oxenbury's *Farmer Duck* (Walker, see page 81) is all about friendship and unselfishness, whereas *The Rainbow Fish* (North/South Books) is about vanity and sharing.

Whenever you try a new book with your children, look for the moral messages it might contain. Can these messages be used to get children thinking about the difference between right and wrong or the effects of their behaviour on other people? In the past, young children have traditionally been regarded as egocentric - unable to take on someone else's viewpoint or understand how somebody else might be feeling. More recent research indicates that this is not the case. Young children are perfectly capable of empathising with others - they simply need to learn that other people do have needs and feelings. A well written and illustrated picture book is good at creating characters we can all associate with. This takes the child one step further towards realising that other people are separate individuals with different but valid life styles and viewpoints. Making these discoveries and learning to empathise with others is an essential aspect of emotional and social development.

MOTIVATION TO LEARN

The Early Learning Goals include motivation to learn as a part of Personal, Social and Emotional Development. Picture books are invaluable when it comes to meeting this goal. A well crafted story told through words and pictures fosters learning without the child even realising it. Even adults will pick up things more effectively through a good story and this is certainly so with the child. As long as you select your books carefully, any story group will help the child develop her interests and motivation to learn about whatever new worlds the picture book might be offering. The other great advantage of picture books in this respect is that there truly is something for everyone. Whatever a child's interests, there will be a matching picture book out there somewhere if you only look hard enough.

From: *Who's Who in Our Street?*

Communication, Language and Literacy

Picture books are obviously essential to the young child's literacy development. There are many different aspects to becoming a reader - from learning to read the words on the page to understanding how a story works. In the end, it is only through hands-on experience that the child absorbs these things. If the child is to become wholly literate, books should be a part of her everyday life.

GETTING TO KNOW BOOKS

In the first instance, the child has to learn how to handle a book. Some children will arrive at your setting with lots of experience of books, others with barely any at all.

Watch how the children in your group treat books and show them any skills that seem to be needed. For instance, demonstrate how to carry a book carefully and how to replace a book in the bookshelf or book box. Give each child a turn so that they can practise the skill for themselves and be ready to repeat this little activity a number of times.

Whenever you share a book, show the children the front cover. Look at the picture and read the name of the book (the title). This will help the child absorb which is the front of the book and which way up it goes - useful knowledge to have when it comes to putting the book away correctly. Watch out for books being dropped, left lying around and generally mistreated. Books are not the toughest of objects and it is never too soon to encourage children to treat them with care and respect.

You may also want to show the children how to turn the pages without crumpling or tearing them. Choose books that make it clear to the young child that there is something interesting to look at when you turn the page. Janet and Alan Ahlberg's *Peepo!* (Puffin) actually enables you to peep through the cut-out hole to see a tantalising detail from the next page. Another good choice is Eric Carle's *Brown Bear, Brown Bear, What Do You See?* (Puffin). To find out which brightly coloured animal he can see, all you have to do is turn the page.

Help the children to become familiar with books by naming all the different parts. Start off at a simple level with *page, cover* and perhaps *picture*. Progress onto *front cover; back cover; end papers* (the brightly coloured pages and inside cover at the beginning and end of the story); *gutter* (the crease at the centre of the book where the two pages join); *spine; words* and *print; title* and the name of the *author* and *illustrator*. With the occasional older child you could also show her the name of the *publisher* and the *price*. Talk about the meaning of these words and why they are printed on the back of the book.

Naming the parts of the book can be a little one-off activity that you slip into the beginning or end of a story session. Alternatively, you can turn it into a mini project. Look out for books that display the part you want to name in a particularly clear or interesting way. For example, Eric Carle's books usually have brightly coloured end papers; try *From Head to Toe* (Puffin). If you want to show children the spine of a book, choose a hardback with the title printed along it. Show older ones how a book is put in a traditional bookshelf so they can think about why the title is written on the spine. Some books show a picture of the author/artist at the back or front of the book. *From Head to Toe* has a little full length photo of Eric Carle, helping to bring alive the concept of the author/illustrator.

As part of getting to know books, it is fun to explore different formats. Show the children board books and paperbacks. Talk about how they are different and why we have board books. Look out for a popular book that comes in different forms and order them from the library. Kaye Umansky's *Pass the Jam, Jim* is published in both mini and regular sizes (Red Fox). Janet and Alan Ahlberg's *Each Peach Pear Plum* (Puffin) is published in board book format, in regular paperback format, in hardback and as a big book (Longman). Show the children that the words and pictures are exactly the same, in spite of the different sizes and forms. Talk about the reasons for all these differences. If you use big books with your group, let the children take it in turns to look at the small version while you read.

Look out also for differently shaped books - tall and thin, short and long, even perfectly square. Lydia Monks' delightful *I Wish I Were a Dog* (Mammoth) is exactly the same shape and size as John Burningham's *Grandpa* (Puffin) but one is printed in landscape format (horizontally) and the other in portrait (vertically). This makes the books look quite different from each other.

For something out of the ordinary, David Pelham's *Sam's Sandwich* (Jonathan Cape) has sandwich-shaped pages while David Wojtowycz's *Oink* (David and Charles) comes complete with cut-out animals attached to the book by different coloured ribbons. All of these books can be read as straight stories to your three-year-olds and explored as different examples of picture books by older ones.

MAKING YOUR OWN BOOK

Making your own book is a lovely way of encouraging children to think about and investigate the structure of the book itself. Try to ensure that your children have enjoyed a variety of different books before introducing the activity. The aim is for the children to plan their book as much as possible - but they can only decide about aspects such as the size and shape of pages if they know what a page is and the various options available to them.

Before making each part of the book, look at a variety of examples and discuss with the children the possibilities. (See box below right.)

You and your children are now ready for the most important bit - the words and the pictures that go inside. The only rule about a picture book is that there are no rules! Have fun choosing and making whatever you want for the content of your picture book.

EXPLORING WHAT'S INSIDE:
WRITTEN LANGUAGE

Investigating what lies inside is probably the most important aspect of getting to know books for the young child. Written language is quite different from spoken language. As you choose books for your group, bear in mind the various styles of language you are introducing. For example, Shirley Hughes' beautifully written *Alfie* stories (Red Fox) use clear, everyday, functional language. Ruth Brown's *The Picnic* (Red Fox) uses poetic language with lots of dramatic adjectives (suitable for the four plus age group). Jez Alborough's *It's the Bear* (Walker) uses short sentences with light-hearted and jolly words. Trish Cooke's unusual *So Much* (Walker) is written in authentic Caribbean speech.

Make sure that you introduce books with dialogue - the words that characters speak. This will help the child get used to the difference between those parts where the story is told by the writer, and those parts where the character speaks his or her

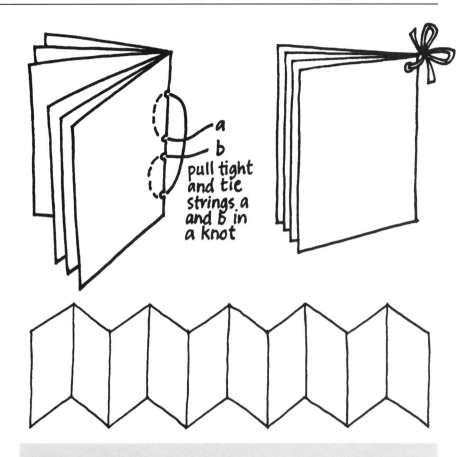

Making your own book

■ Look at the covers on a range of different books. How do they differ from the pages? Point out that the cover is made from stiff card. Name and compare hardbacks and paperbacks. Talk about the reasons for different types of cover: most libraries buy hardbacks because they will last whereas paperbacks are cheaper for families who do not need such hardwearing books.

■ Look at the pictures on the covers. Talk about how they link with the story or the theme, to help you guess what the book is about. Look at the titles; the colour, the size of the letters, where on the cover the title is written. If the children are ready, talk about the reasons - for instance, the title has to be printed in large, clear letters so that you can see it easily. Lydia Monks' *I Wish I Were a Dog* is a good example of a typical cover. The title is clearly written in black letters at the top. The name of the author / illustrator is written in smaller letters at the bottom (not quite such important information as the title). The picture shows a fed-up looking Kitty, the central character in the story. This tells us straightaway that the story is about a disgruntled cat. Take the discussion as far as your children are ready for.

■ As much as possible, encourage the children to take part in cutting out the pages and attaching them to make the book. Look at where the pages are joined to the cover on a selection of books and then choose a method of joining the pages for your own book. The most authentic technique is to fold pieces of paper in two and sew them together. You could also tie the pages by punching a hole in one corner or create a concertina book (see diagrams).

own words. The cleverly written dialogue in John Burningham's *Mr Gumpy's Outing* (Puffin) makes this classic an excellent choice. It is easy to hear Mr Gumpy's voice (and the voice of every impatient adult) in words such as *'All right then, but don't muck about.'* In contrast, the straightforward storytelling parts include sentences such as *'and they all fell into the water with a splash'* - a different style of language to reflect a different purpose.

Young children also need to become familiar with traditional story language and books from the past. *The Little Red Hen and the Ear of Wheat* by Mary Finch (Barefoot Books) and *The Gigantic Turnip* by Aleksei Tolstoy and Niamh Sharkey (Barefoot Books) are both re-tellings of traditional tales. Gene Zion's *Harry the Dirty Dog* and Anita Hewett's *Mrs Mopple's Washing Line* were first published in the 1950s and 60s, but they still have an enormous appeal for today's generation of children.

For older children, try Joyce Lancaster Brisley's *Milly Molly Mandy* stories. Written in the 1920s, they give a flavour of earlier times, as does Dorothy Edwards' *My Naughty Little Sister* stories from the 1950s and 60s. The language of some Beatrix Potter books is still accessible for young children. Try *Appley Dapply's Nursery Rhymes* and *Cecily Parsley's Nursery Rhymes*, both genuine Victorian picture books.

Of course, young children will not be able to recognise, analyse or describe different styles and purposes of language. Nor will they have a clear understanding of history, or be able to set a book in its historical context. They do, however, absorb what they see and hear. If the young child's

experience of books includes some from the past, the later task of reading classic novels, poetry, plays and studying historical documents comes much more easily. The wider an experience the child has at a young age, the better she is able to cope with all forms of written language as an adult.

Once your children have enjoyed a number of traditional tales and nursery rhymes, it is time to introduce some of the picture books that play with traditional themes. Janet and

Down the lane...

"Moo!"

From: *Farmer Duck*

Alan Ahlberg's *Each Peach Pear Plum* is a classic example. You don't have to know your nursery rhymes to enjoy it, but it adds another dimension when you can recognise characters and names from other stories. Jonathan Allan's *Chicken Licken* (Picture Corgi) is a clever version of the original; the story is told in straightforward language, with an additional (and hilarious) running commentary from the animals added in speech bubbles. As well as being great fun, stories such as this one show that you can play around with a story - something that many children do for themselves from a surprisingly early age.

Another means of exploring books is to concentrate on a theme, genre or single author/illustrator. You can either gather a number of books to fit in with the theme you are looking at or choose a genre such as nursery rhymes, fairy stories, humorous stories, ABCs or lift-the-flap books. As

part of helping your children learn about the author and illustrator, introduce several different books by the same author. Shirley Hughes, Eric Carle, Nick Butterworth, John Burningham and Rod Campbell are all popular writers/illustrators who have several books in print. Display your book collection in the book corner so the children can look at them whenever they wish.

A HAPPY ENDING?

One cannot talk about written language and the content of a book without mentioning how the story makes you feel. Language style and the mood of a story go hand in hand. The light-hearted words in Jez Alborough's *It's the Bear* result in a story to make you laugh and feel jolly. Ruth Brown's dramatic prose in *The Picnic* contributes to a feeling of danger and fear. Always remember that in giving your children a range of written language styles, you are at the same time giving them a range of emotional experiences - an essential aspect of getting to know stories. For a more detailed look at the emotional aspects of story, see pages 7-9.

LEARNING HOW A STORY WORKS

A story does not just consist of the language and pictures. The *structure* of the story is also important. This includes story elements such as the *beginning*, the *ending*, the *central characters* and the *setting* of the story.

This may seem a tall order for little ones, but children do start to absorb a sense of story from the very first moment they look at a book. The experienced adult has no difficulty working out who a story is about (the central character) or where the story is taking place (the setting). Because these story elements are so obvious to us, we can sometimes forget that the young child still has to learn - and that she can only do so through lots of story experiences.

The following are perhaps the most fundamental elements of story structure:

◆ **CENTRAL CHARACTER:** picture books are an excellent means of helping the young child recognise the central character. Take *The Very Hungry Caterpillar*. The words *tell* you all about him while the pictures *show* you what he looks like. When his name and picture keep popping up on each page, it helps the child to realise that this is the character the story is about - this is the one to look out for.

Choose books with a strong and accessible central character. Gene Zion's *Harry the Dirty Dog*, John Burningham's *Mr Gumpy*, Eric Hill's *Spot the Dog* (Puffin), Shirley Hughes' *Alfie*, Mick Inkpen's *Kipper* (Hodder), David McKee's *Elmer the Elephant* are just a few of the many delightful characters to be found in picture books. These are all characters who have had more than one story written about them so that you can read other books from the series. Try to match characters to the interests of your children so that they can identify with them. Help the children to focus on the main characters by:

◆ naming them and talking about them;

◆ describing their appearance and personality;

◆ emphasising their importance in role-play activities;

◆ writing about them;

◆ drawing and painting them.

Make a display of books, drawings, paintings and writing for a particular character. Many popular

story figures such as *Spot the Dog, Elmer the Elephant, Thomas the Tank Engine* and *Winnie-the-Pooh* have generated a wide variety of merchandise. This can be another entry into looking at a particular character. Gather a collection of greetings cards, badges, tins of pasta shapes, sweets, stationery and so on. Encourage the children to bring in items from home and add these to your display.

◆ **SETTINGS:** the setting of a story is less obvious than the central character, but very important. In novels for older children and adults, the writer sets the scene with lots of landscape description. Wordy descriptions are too much for little ones, but the picture can *show* where the story is taking place. With a picture to look at, the child is

When We Went to the Park

From: The Nursery Collection

easily able to absorb a complex and detailed setting for a story.

There is no shortage of picture books with beautifully drawn and interesting backgrounds. The pictures in *Each Peach Pear Plum* show the gentle, rolling English

countryside; Mairi Hedderwick's pictures in her *Katie Morag* stories (Bodley Head) include striking, panoramic scenes of a Scottish island; Lynley Dodd's *Hairy Maclary* and *Slinki Malinki* series (Puffin) are set against an urban backdrop, suitable for the adventures of a town dwelling cat and dog. If you can provide books with a variety of different settings, the child will gradually learn that *where* a story happens is important and interesting.

◆ **ENDINGS:** endings are crucial to a story. It is important for the child to realise that stories have endings. This is one of the main impulses that keeps the reader going right through to the end of the book. There are two ways in which picture books are useful for helping children to learn about endings: picture books often have clever, funny or surprising endings; and the book itself helps the child realise that the story has finished. You reach the last page and there is nowhere else to go beyond the back cover. Closing the book slowly and deliberately and laying it in your lap is a small but significant gesture in helping the child realise that the story has come to an end.

Endings come in all shapes and sizes, particularly in a picture book with both pictures and words at the disposal of the author/illustrator. The ending of Philippe Dupasquier's *Dear Daddy* (Puffin) is so emotionally significant that he uses just pictures. Words would somehow be inappropriate. On the other hand, Pat Hutchins' *Rosie's Walk* has a safe, comforting ending, suitable for a story that includes a predatory fox. Jez Alborough's *Washing Line* is funny, with a last-minute surprise in keeping with the flavour of the whole book. Jan Ormerod uses large letters and heavy type to emphasise the words that make up the ending of *Who's Who in Our Street?*

As you choose books for your children, be aware of the many different types of endings you can offer. Talk about the ending. Ask the children if they can remember what happens or to predict what they think is going to happen if a story is new to them. Use a variety of words to describe the ending and how it makes you feel: surprising, funny, happy, jolly, safe. Try thinking up some different endings. Some children may simply re-tell the original, others will take off on a flight of fantasy. Either way, you are helping them to focus on the concept of the ending.

CONVERSATION

A picture book makes the perfect trigger for conversation with young children. Children learn a huge amount from chatting with adults about anything and everything. Although it is sometimes frustrating for the story to be interrupted, it is important to stop, listen and respond. When you are managing a large group, you may feel limited as to how much interruption you can allow. For this reason, it is well worth trying to hold as many small story groups as possible. Always remember that anyone can pick up and share a book with young children - the perfect activity for visitors and helpers. Draft in lots of parents, grandparents and teenagers on work experience and convince them that simply reading and chatting with the children is immeasurably valuable.

While all conversation between adults and children is valuable, book-based discussions have some special and unique qualities:

◆ To begin with, you are all sitting still, looking and listening - a set-up that is much more conducive to good, extended conversation than playing with a ball or watching a video. Everyone in the group is looking at the same picture and listening to the same words, which

can help you to make sense of what the child is saying (and vice versa). This can be particularly useful with a very young child, a child with special needs or a child who does not have English as a first language.

"How goes the work?"
"Quack!"

"How goes the work?"
"Quack!"

From: *Farmer Duck*

◆ A story can only say so much. Even a full-length adult novel leaves great chunks to the imagination. Older children and adults understand this and fill in the gaps almost without thinking. Little children do not and will often wonder about what is going on 'behind' the story. Look out for questions such as *'Where's the Mummy gone?'* or *'When did Timmy go to the doctor?'* Gradually, the child will learn that these questions are irrelevant to the story - but in the meantime, make the most of the opportunity to help the child make sense of both the story and the world in general. If you and the child have time to meander away from the story, the question about Timmy and the doctor could lead you into all sorts of interesting areas of learning.

A picture book provides numerous opportunities for misunderstanding. This seems an

odd point to add to a list of useful things about book-based conversation. However, as long as there is somebody on hand to answer questions, children learn a huge amount from their errors of understanding.

The combination of words and pictures is a common cause of confusion. Often, the words say one thing while the pictures seem to be saying something completely different. Young children are also not very experienced at 'reading' pictures and sometimes they misinterpret what they see. Fortunately, young children are good at sensing when something doesn't seem quite right and they will ask - particularly when they know that the adult is receptive to their questions.

Book-based conversation can grow and develop from one story session to the next. Re-read a popular book as often as you can and look out for the same topics of conversation coming up again and again. This is an extremely useful opportunity for the children to build their understanding and develop their language skills.

THE MECHANICS OF READING AND WRITING

Preparation for reading begins from the moment the child first looks at a book. The child will absorb the print on the page even though she does not understand its meaning. Letters, common letter clusters (such as *thr*) and common words (such as *the* or *why*) will gradually become visually familiar to the child so that when she starts to read, she is working with something she has seen again and again.

For this reason, it is important to let the children see the printed page as much as possible. Try the following to make the most of opportunities:

◆ Have the children sitting as close to you as possible and hold up the book. Read upside down or sideways so that they can see the print.
◆ Make sure the children in a small group are sitting next to you and can look at the pages while you read.
◆ Occasionally point to words as you read, to help the children link your spoken words with the print on the page.
◆ Talk about aspects such as *'reading the words on the page'* and *'turning over the page so that I can read the next bit of the story.'*

Look out for books with repeating text. Not only do the children love familiarity and the chance to join in, they also give the opportunity for the child to hear and see the same printed letters and words, over and over again. Try Penny Dale's *Ten in the Bed* (Walker) and Eric Carle's *Brown Bear, Brown Bear, What Do You See?* (Puffin) for little ones. Try Anita Hewett's *Mrs Mopple's Washing Line* (Red Fox) for your four- year-olds.

While all books with printed text have their role to play in reading development, some are aimed specifically at helping the child learn the different sounds that make up our language. There are many alphabet books focusing on the 26 letters of the alphabet and the sounds they

represent - usually through identifying the initial sound of a word.

The picture book is ideal for introducing a letter because it can include a picture of an object beginning with a particular sound, the written name of the object and the symbol for the sound. For example, a picture of a mouse, the printed word mouse and the symbol 'm', preferably in both lower and upper case (Mm).

Choose books that clearly show the letter symbols and introduce as wide a variety as possible. Many favourite characters have their own ABC. Egmont Children's Books publish *Postman Pat's ABC* and *ABC with Winnie-the-Pooh*. Maisy the Mouse has her own ABC (Walker) as does Nick Butterworth's *Percy the Park Keeper* (Collins). The familiarity of a well-known character can make a useful bridge, particularly for the more reluctant child.

If you prefer a good, general alphabet book, *Flora McDonnell's ABC* (Walker) has lovely illustrations and is a good size for using with groups. For something a little different, try Lucy Micklethwait's *I Spy: an Alphabet in Art*. Through the challenge of looking for something beginning with each of the 26 letters of the alphabet, the child is introduced to various well-known paintings. You can also look out for alphabets to fit in with your theme, such as Philippa-Alys Browne's *African Animals ABC* (Barefoot Books).

Rhyming texts, jingles and nursery rhymes are also important in helping the child to recognise the sounds that make up our language. The rhythms of a nursery rhyme break words into their constituent sounds (*tu-pen-ny*) - a useful skill when it comes to reading. Nursery rhymes, poems, songs and jingles are a popular theme for picture books and there are many to choose from. Iona Opie's *My Very First Mother Goose* is a beautifully illustrated collection of traditional and more unusual rhymes (Walker). *Down by the River* is an anthology of rhymes and songs from the Caribbean (Mammoth).

A number of picture books have rhyming texts. Lynley Dodds' *Hairy Maclary* series (Puffin) has wonderful rhymes and rhythms, as do Kaye Umansky's *Pass the Jam, Jim* and *You Can Swim Jim* (Red Fox). All of these books are suitable for use with the whole pre-school age range.

WORDS, WORDS, WORDS

Picture books provide a huge source of new vocabulary for young children. Some books set out to introduce new words. Many favourite characters have their own word books, such as *Spot's Big Book of Words* (Puffin.) Others include sections or elements designed to introduce new words, such as Shirley Hughes' *Bouncing* (Walker), with its page of action words at the end. Some books emphasise certain words through repetition.

The best word learning opportunities occur spontaneously. The child happens not to know a word but the context of the story and the pictures make that word meaningful to her. As the book is re-read, her exposure to the new word is repeated and she gradually and naturally absorbs its meaning into her mental storehouse of vocabulary. This is not something you can plan for, but it will happen if you read lots of books and repeat favourites as often as possible.

Because of the context of the story and the pictures, the child can easily take one or two unfamiliar words in her stride. Interestingly, it is relatively unusual for a young child to ask what a word means, perhaps because the context of the story makes it unnecessary. A famous example is Beatrix Potter's Peter Rabbit, who is *soporific* after eating too many lettuces. Obviously, this is an unfamiliar word, but the picture shows the child perfectly clearly what the word means.

As part of helping children to expand their store of words, look out for books that cover different word groups - nouns, adjectives, verbs, adverbs and prepositions. While you would not name or discuss word types with young children, the groups can still be used as a framework for ensuring that the children get a wide variety of word experience.

NAMING WORDS: any word book gives lots of nouns or naming words. Alphabet books can also give lots of names. Books with a particular theme, such as autumn, will usually include a range of new words.

DESCRIBING WORDS: many describing words or adjectives are introduced in concept books. Size, colour, shape, contrasts (hot/cold, heavy/light) are all popular themes for picture books. Shirley Hughes' *Nursery Collection* (Walker) includes most of them - 'Bathwater's hot, seawater's cold'; 'Green lettuce, green peas, green shade from green trees'; 'Squeeze through narrow spaces, run through wide'. As well as introducing all these concepts to the child, books such as this one give lots of words that tell us what something is like. And as with all picture books, there is the advantage of a picture to show you the meaning of the word.

ACTION WORDS: Shirley Hughes' *Bouncing* (Walker) focuses on action and has a page of action words (verbs) with little pictures at the end. Eric Carle's *From Head to Toe* is all about different movements. Both of these books can be used as a starting point for trying out different action words. Use the accompanying pictures to help the children understand the meaning of the word.

POSITION WORDS: *Rosie's Walk* and Penny Dale's *Ten Play Hide and Seek* both use lots of position words (prepositions). See page 56 for further ideas on highlighting and exploring the position words in *Rosie's Walk*.

WRITING

As we have seen, there are a huge number of learning opportunities to be gained from a picture book - and every single one of these will contribute to the child's development as a writer. A child may or may not be able to produce her own writing by the time she leaves your setting. However, if you have shared with her lots of carefully chosen picture books, you will have given her invaluable help and preparation towards this essential skill:

◆ The opportunity to look at and absorb print will help the child when it comes to knowing what a letter looks like, as well as reproducing letter clusters and words. The child who reads tends to be a more accurate speller later in life - a long and complex process that begins as soon as she first looks at a book.

◆ Listening to a wide variety of stories helps the child gather lots of inspiration. It can be surprising how early a child will draw on the stories she has listened to when she comes to tell (and later write) her own stories.

◆ Written language, like spoken language, is dependent on words. Obviously, a wide vocabulary is important if the child is to express herself easily and successfully in writing. Not only do picture books play a role in increasing general vocabulary, they also offer 'story vocabulary' - the kind of poetic or story-based language one tends to find only in books.

◆ Learning how a story works also helps the child to structure her own stories: an interesting beginning, a clear central character, a strong ending. All these story elements are first introduced to the child through picture books.

DEAR ALL—
WE MISS YOU!
WISH YOU WERE
HERE. THE BEACH
IS GREAT!
LOTS OF LOVE —
BIDDIE   X
BILL   X
BEA   X
BUGS   X
BOO BOO   X
(and BEAR) X

MAGGIE, MEL, MICKY,
MOLLY, JENNY, JOSH,
JAKE, JOCK + CAT
c/o MRS. BLUE
19 THE AVENUE
BROOKLANDS

From: *Who's Who in Our Street?*

Mathematical Development

Mathematical development depends on skills such as counting, sequencing, sorting, matching and the ability to work with shape, space, size and measurement.

Picture books have an important role to play in helping all aspects of the child's mathematical development. As with other areas of learning, mathematical information can be disseminated both through stories and in the form of the concept book - a book which takes a theme such as number, shape or size and explores it through words and pictures.

The following sections look at how picture books can help the development of some key mathematical skills.

NUMBER
Number books:
Number and counting are popular themes for picture books. The combination of words and pictures creates an ideal format through which to present number to young children: they can count the number of items in the picture, hear the name of the quantity as it is read aloud (one, two, three) and see the number symbol written on the page (1, 2, 3). This is yet another occasion when the repeatability of the picture book is useful. You and your children can return to the book again and again, and take as long as you need to count each quantity before you turn the page.

The structure of the book is also helpful in presenting the sequence of numbers. The pages are separate but follow each other in order, just like the order of numbers. Counting books usually make good use of this structure by devoting a single page to each number group. As you progress through the book, turning the pages one by one, so you progress through the number sequence.
The wide choice of counting books

available means that you can usually find something to match the child's interests. Many characters have their own counting books. Try the publisher Egmont for *Winnie the Pooh, Postman Pat* and *Sesame Street*, amongst others. It is also worth looking out for counting books by author/illustrators who have proved to be popular with your children on previous occasions. If your group has enjoyed Rod Campbell's *Dear Zoo* (Puffin), they should also like his *Farm 123* (Puffin). If Shirley Hughes' stories have gone down well, try *Lucy and Tom's 1 2 3* (Puffin).

A book such as *Farm 123* is perfect for introducing young children to number. For older ones who know their numbers, choose books that provide a challenge and encourage them to use their counting skills. Satoshi Kitamura's *When Sheep Cannot Sleep* (Red Fox) is a number book with a difference. There is great fun to be had in spotting whatever we are meant to count on each page - not always obvious at first glance. Clare Beaton's *One Moose, Twenty Mice* (Barefoot Books) is another unusual example with stunning felt applique illustrations. It takes us from 1 to 20 and on each page there is the additional challenge of spotting the cat amongst the different groups of animals.

Addition and subtraction:
Also for older children, there are a few books that introduce the mathematical skills of addition and subtraction. Sally Crabtree's *One Spinning Spider* (David and Charles) includes a spider finger puppet on a ribbon. The child herself adds the spider to each page so that she can actively take part in the process of addition. For the occasional child who is ready, you can also introduce mathematical symbols through the sums printed on each page: 5 + 1 = 6.

Counting opportunities:
Along with specific number books, look out for counting opportunities within stories. *Mr Gumpy's Outing* is a good example of a story that does not set out to be a counting book, but lends itself readily to counting activities. With children who can count, you can use the pictures in books to practise and consolidate their skills. Count details such as the number of cows in a field, the number of buttons on somebody's jacket or the number of people in a crowd scene. The pages can also be counted and you can show older children the page numbers, chapters and index in an adult's book.

SEQUENCING
Counting depends on recognising and remembering a sequence - in this case, the sequence of numbers. A sequence is made up of two or more objects or events placed in a successive order. All stories follow the basic sequence of beginning, middle and end while many revolve around a sequence of events. The structure that makes *Mr Gumpy's Outing* useful for counting depends on the order of animals that builds up throughout the story.

Aleksei Tolstoy's *The Gigantic Turnip* is another excellent story for introducing young children to sequence. Like *Mr Gumpy's Outing*, the groups of animals build up one after the other until the climax of the story is reached. Barefoot Books publish a simple version of this traditional tale, with beautiful and unusual illustrations by Niamh Sharkey.

One of the best ways of helping young children to explore the sequence of a story is through role play (see *Mr Gumpy's Outing* role-play activity, page 35). This gives the children first-hand experience of how the structure is built up. You and your children can also use a story as the starting point for a picture sequence to display in

Mathematical Development

your setting (see *Washing Line* number sequence activity, page 47).

MATCHING AND SORTING

Counting, matching and sorting are inextricably linked, and most number books are based on a clear sorting procedure. The pictures usually show the items sorted into groups - one dog, two cats, three monkeys, four sheep. If you are able to provide a counting activity based on a particular number book, this will give the child a first-hand experience of sorting and counting as a follow-up to what she has seen within the book (see *Ten, Nine, Eight* 'Body counting' activity, page 60).

Having counted the groups of objects, the next step is for the child to match the quantity with its name and symbol (one and 1). Most counting books give the child a good introduction to this process by placing the quantity side by side with its symbol - a picture of four sheep next to the symbol 4.

Both sorting and matching depend on being able to identify similarities and differences - the four sheep in the above counting example go together because they are all sheep; the group of sheep can be matched with the symbol 4 because they both represent the same number. As we have already seen, picture books have a massive potential to develop the child's knowledge of similarity and difference (see 'Similarities, differences, pattern and change' page 20).

If you want a picture book that focuses specifically on matching and sorting, try William Benedict's clever *Bedtime for Little Pandas* (Walker). The pandas' house has to be tidied up before bedtime. This involves both matching and sorting. Each item has to be matched with its empty space, which naturally involves adding it to a group of similar items - the mug goes on the empty hook along with the two other mugs, for example.

SHAPE AND DIMENSION

In order to identify similarity and difference, the child must be able to recognise different criteria such as shape and dimension. Again, the picture book has enormous potential for introducing the child to all these different environmental properties, both through story and through concept or theme books.

Shape: this is a common criteria for sorting and matching and an important aspect of Mathematical Development. Some picture books use story to explore shape in general terms. John Burningham's *Little Cloud* (Puffin) transforms into all kinds of different shapes while his *Mixed-Up Chameleon* (Puffin) changes colour and size as well as shape. Other books look more specifically at geometric shapes and their properties. Stella Blackstone's *Bear in a Square* (Barefoot Books) offers the challenge of a shape to find on each page. Dayle Ann Dodds' *All Shapes and Sizes* encourages children to see the geometric shapes all around them by building pictures out of triangles, squares, rectangles and circles. Use this book as a starting point for making your own shape pictures.

Dimension: properties such as size also lend themselves well to words and pictures. Many picture books that set out to explore height, width and size do so through opposites or contrasts. Setting pictures of large and small, tall and short, fat and thin or narrow and wide alongside each other shows the child the quality and helps them to focus on that quality through comparison. 'Opposites' are almost as popular a theme for the picture book as number and an opposites concept book can be used as the starting point for activities based on contrasting sizes and dimensions (see *The Nursery Collection*, 'Environmental qualities'

and 'Exploring the environment' activities).

As with all other mathematical elements, dimension and contrast also crop up time and time again embedded within a story. Martin Waddell's *Can't You Sleep Little Bear?* (Walker) features a big bear and a small bear. Pat Hutchins' *Titch* stories (Red Fox) are based on Titch being smaller and shorter than his siblings. The bear in Jez Alborough's *Where's the Bear?* (Walker) fills the pages in comparison with the little boy and his toy teddy bear.

OTHER MATHEMATICAL PROPERTIES

While shape and size are the most obvious mathematical elements apart from number, maths is all around us. The perspective the child witnesses when she looks at the panoramic scenes in Mairi Hedderwick's *Katie Morag* stories (Red Fox) is mathematical. So is the farmyard scene in the opening pages of *Rosie's Walk*, showing the position of each farmyard feature. Benedict Blathwayt's *The Runaway Train* (Red Fox) deals with speed and distance. John Burningham's *Avocado Baby* (Red Fox) is about strength and weight as well as size.

As part of your provision for Mathematical Development, be aware of the wide range of mathematical concepts that emerge from stories. Even where they are incidental to the story, they offer an important foundation and can be used as the starting point for looking more closely at a mathematical element.

From: *Who's Who in Our Street?*

Knowledge and Understanding of the World

This area of learning covers a wide range of knowledge, skills and capabilities. At the pre-school stage, the main aim is to develop the child's ability to make sense of the world around her. This provides a foundation for all aspects of life, including the history, geography, science, information and communication technology and design technology that she will study in later years.

THE ROLE OF BOOKS IN EXPLORING THE WORLD

It is essential that the child has lots of hands-on opportunities to explore her surroundings, both through free play and carefully planned activities. When it comes to discovering and learning about all aspects of the environment, there is no substitute for actual experience. However, this does not mean that books provide second-rate learning opportunities, even though they could be regarded as one step removed from real life. The picture book has some special advantages when it comes to learning about the world:

◆ A good story is an excellent medium through which to offer information to young children. Knowledge is often much more likely to stay with the child when it is received within the context of a story.

◆ Skilful picture book writers and artists are clever at highlighting interesting and important ideas, themes, elements or bodies of knowledge. Even a complex book such as *Who's Who in Our Street?* (see pages 75-82) can only show a small part of the whole picture. If that small part has been chosen carefully and presented with skill, it will give the child excellent opportunities to increase her knowledge and

understanding of whatever themes are central to the story.

◆ A book is a quick, convenient and easy way of offering facts and information. In some cases, a theme or concept is much easier to explore via a picture book than in real life. Try explaining the idea of time passing concurrently for two people in separate places to a four-year-old, without a book such as *Dear Daddy* to help you (see pages 69-74) - possible, but much more difficult!

◆ In comparison with real life a book is simple. Even the most complex and detailed picture book offers information in a simplified form compared to the ever changing, many layered world surrounding the child.

◆ The words and pictures in a picture book give double the communication possibilities because the book can both tell us and show us how things are. While a picture is generally easier for the child to comprehend than words, the text of the book can steer the child towards noticing certain things in the picture. The picture, meanwhile, can offer all kinds of information that would be too wordy for the young child if it were a part of the text. When it comes to extending the child's knowledge and understanding of the world, this is invaluable.

SOMETHING FOR EVERYONE

The title for this area of learning - Knowledge and Understanding of the World - covers just about everything. Fortunately, picture books also cover just about everything! The following list is a short, random selection of some classic and well-known picture

books. When you look at the topics, themes and knowledge areas they offer, it is a reminder of just how much information picture books have to give - and all in a form that is highly accessible to the young child:

• Pat Hutchins' *Rosie's Walk* (Puffin - see pages 55-59) highlights position words as Rosie makes her way around the farmyard. The pictures present the topography and characteristic features of a farmyard.

• Philippe Dupasquier's *Dear Daddy* (Puffin - see pages 69-74) explores time passing concurrently for two people living in separate places. Both pictures and words give a view of day-to-day family life and the pictures show the passing seasons and seasonal weather.

• Mairi Hedderwick's *Katie Morag* stories (Bodley Head) give lots of information about life on a Scottish island and explore the relationships between neighbours and family members in a small, remote community.

• Janet and Alan Ahlberg's *Each Peach Pear Plum* (Puffin) makes creative use of nursery rhyme/fairy tale characters and rhyming words. The pictures use the traditional English countryside as a backdrop for the events that take place.

• Angela Royston's *The Story of...* series (Kingfisher) explores large vehicles, their purpose, how they are used, what they look like and the names of their different parts.

• Shirley Hughes' *Lucy and Tom's Christmas* (Puffin) looks at numerous aspects of a modern, urban Christmas as experienced by two young children.

When it comes to choosing picture books to help a child develop her

Knowledge and Understanding of the World

knowledge and understanding of the world, the ideal book will tally with the child's interests and work on two levels:

i) confirming what the child already knows about the theme or topic

ii) leading her on to a new level of understanding.

For example, if you have a building site near your setting and the children develop an interest in what is happening, you can show them Angela Royston's *Story of a Digger* (Kingfisher). This wonderful book contains all kinds of information that they can match with what they have seen and heard, as well as broadening their knowledge with new facts such as what the inside of the cab looks like or the names of the different parts.

DISCOVERING THE PAST

As well as exploring the material world, the Early Learning Goals require children to find out about past and present events in their own lives, those of their families and other people they know. This is the beginning of learning about history. There are not a huge number of picture books with a historical flavour, but those that are available make an excellent means of presenting the past in a spontaneous and natural way. The charming pictures in Janet and Alan Ahlberg's *Peepo!* (Puffin) show a family during the second world war, with all the little domestic details lovingly depicted for the children to notice and observe. Penny Ives' *Granny's Quilt* (Puffin - suitable for four plus) takes a different approach in that it provides a bridge between past and present. Granny's patchwork quilt is

Mandy series (for older ones) was written when Grandma was little. Dorothy Edwards' *My Naughty Little Sister* books date from when parents were little. Both stories reflect the language, lifestyles and attitudes of the 1920s and 1960s respectively, because that is when they were written. Make a start at putting them into a historical context for older ones by telling the children that these stories were written when Granny/Mummy was little. It is never too early to offer a taste of earlier times through a carefully chosen story, even if your children are too young to have much sense of the past.

SIMILARITIES, DIFFERENCES, PATTERN AND CHANGE

Another Early Learning Goal for this area with a special link to picture

Whose are those socks hanging on the washing line?

asked the elephant.

It is impossible to cater for every child's individual tastes, but you can look out for general interests and also encourage parents to follow up a particular interest at home. Use the Internet to keep up with what is available, or treat yourself to an afternoon in a good book shop or library from time to time. It is always worth checking Dorling Kindersley's list of publications, particularly if you are trying to find books on specialised subjects. Their hallmark clear photographs on bright white backgrounds are great for young children, even when the text and annotations are beyond them.

made out of all the different dresses she has worn throughout her life and she uses it to tell her story, from girlhood to the present day. Even if your children are not ready to take on board this concept of 'the past', they will still absorb and retain all kinds of visual information from these books - information that will inform their discovery of history later in life.

Books that date from an earlier time can also help the child's historical awareness. Beatrix Potter's stories are genuine Victorian picture books with the language and flavour of her times; Joyce Lancaster Brisley's *Milly Molly*

books is: 'look closely at similarities, differences, patterns and change.' These concepts are the stuff that stories are made of, whether they are central to a story or whether they make up just a part.

Similarity and difference: although they are separate concepts, similarity and difference are, nevertheless, inextricably linked. David McKee's *Elmer* (Red Fox) is a good example of a book that revolves around both themes. Elmer the patchwork elephant is startlingly different from all the other elephants. The story tells of his efforts to change himself so that he looks similar to the rest of his herd. Apart from the social and emotional development issues raised by the story, the words and pictures give the child lots of information about the nature of similarity and difference.

Even where an author does not set out to explore similarity or difference as central themes, they are often present in some form or another:

• *The Very Hungry Caterpillar* (see pages 50-54) is a completely different creature by the end of the story.

• Sophie's garden in *Dear Daddy* is similar from page to page in that it is the same garden, yet different each time because of the effects of the seasonal weather.

Nursery Collection, see pages 64-68) is just one example.

Change: change is inextricably linked to similarity and difference. In all the story book examples given above, the differences are dependent on change. The Very Hungry Caterpillar is different by the end of the book because he goes through a series of changes; the garden in *Dear Daddy* is the same garden but looks different each time because of the changes wrought by the seasons; in wanting to look the same as the other elephants, the different *Elmer* tries to change himself.

Apart from giving the child numerous examples of change within a story, the picture book can condense change. This enables the child to take changes on board much more easily than in life. For example, a butterfly takes months to develop from egg to

traditional pattern with the repetition that young children love and can learn so much from. *Dear Zoo* (page 29), *Grandpa's Handkerchief* (page 25), *Mr Gumpy's Outing* (page 34) *Washing Line* (page 45) and *Farmer Duck* (page 81) all use a set format that is repeated over and over again until the climax of the story is reached. Although we tend to think of pattern as something visual, a picture book can immerse the child in this different form of pattern, adding yet another layer to the child's growing understanding.

While it is easy to find picture books with a clear pattern to the plot, it is harder to find books that focus specifically on pattern. One example is Nick Sharratt's clever and funny *My Mum and Dad Make Me Laugh* (Walker). Dad likes stripes, Mum likes spots and everything they wear, eat and do depends on whether it is stripy

They're mine said the flamingo.

From: *Washing Line*

• The handkerchiefs in *Grandpa's Handkerchief* are all similar in shape and size yet different in colour.

The examples given above are all, first and foremost, story books. Even where the theme is central, as in Elmer, the information is disseminated through a story. A different type of book for the pre-school child is the concept or theme book. This is where words and pictures are used to present the theme in a clear and deliberate way. Opposites and contrasts are a popular theme for this kind of book and there are plenty to choose from - Shirley Hughes' *Bathwater's Hot* (from *The*

adulthood - too long for many young children to witness as a complete process. In *The Very Hungry Caterpillar*, however, the child can trace the butterfly's life-cycle from beginning to end in a short and manageable space of time. She can also go back to the story again and again, to enable her to build layers of understanding about whatever the book has to offer.

Pattern: even the simplest story follows a plot, which is a type of pattern. This is what makes the story a story, rather than just a slice of life. Many children's stories follow a very

or spotty. As a contrast to colourful patterns, the little boy's favourite is plain grey. This clever and satisfying story proves that you can find a good picture book on just about any topic, theme or idea in the world!

Physical Development

Physical Development is the area of learning with perhaps the least obvious link to picture books. Nevertheless, the book is an object that has to be handled and, with the huge range of choice available, you can sometimes find a book to use as the starting point for physical activities.

HANDLING A BOOK

In the Communication, Language and Literacy section under the heading 'Getting to know books', we looked at

movements. Try the wonderful *Sam's Sandwich* by David Pelham (Red Fox). Although this is a flap book, the flaps have to be unfolded rather than simply lifted, making it much more challenging to use.

Most books offer clear feedback to the child if she does not handle them with care. If she does not turn the pages one by one, she will miss parts of the book. If she does not use controlled movements, the paper will tear. Although board books are useful for

(Walker). For a book that is designed specifically for physical activity, try Zita Newcombe's *Toddlerobics* (Walker).

Another lovely book based on movement is Eric Carle's *From Head to Toe* (Puffin). The large, brightly coloured pictures show children and animals making different movements and highlights parts of the body at the same time. The children will have great fun arching their backs like the cat, or scratching their heads like the gorilla in the pictures.

Rosie the hen went for a walk

From: *Rosie's Walk*

how to handle a book. Knowing how to handle a book is an important part of developing literacy. From the Physical Development viewpoint, handling books demands control of fine movements. Carrying the book, opening it, closing it and turning pages are all refined physical activities that will help the child develop hand/eye co-ordination. The many novelty books available also offer some useful opportunities for the child to develop hand movement. Lifting the flaps in *Dear Zoo* or Eric Hill's *Spot the Dog* books (Puffin) is a simple activity that even the youngest child can engage in. For older children, there are books demanding more delicate

your youngest children, it is important that they graduate onto paper pages as soon as possible.

MOVEMENT ACTIVITIES

Picture books are full of movement and activity. For the young child, it is fun to bring the movement alive by using books as a starting point for physical activities. For your youngest children, try Shirley Hughes' *Bouncing* (Walker) or Helen Oxenbury's *All Fall Down and Clap Hands* (Walker). Older children will enjoy acting out the movements in Michael Rosen and Helen Oxenbury's version of the traditional *We're Going on a Bear Hunt*

MOVEMENT IN EVERYTHING

Of course, as with language, movement comes into everything the children do. Quite apart from turning the pages or trying out the actions in a story, the child uses movement with every book-based activity, from painting and role play to sorting, matching and carrying out a science experiment. Even sitting in a group and listening to a story is important. For the young child, the control needed to sit quietly is perhaps the greatest physical challenge of all.

Creative Development

Creative Development covers the visual arts: drawing, painting, printing, collage, model making; dance, drama and role play; making up stories and poems and all forms of singing and music. Picture books themselves are works of art, made up from the two creative media of language and pictures. They can also be used as the inspiration for a number of creative activities.

DIFFERENT STYLES OF PICTURE

Picture book illustrations offer the young child regular access to pictures. This is an important part of the child's visual education and your choice of books can offer a wide variety of visual experiences and artistic styles - from the 'painterly' approach of Ruth Brown to the surreal paintings of Anthony Browne or the light-hearted, cartoony flavour of Janet and Alan Ahlberg. Picture book artists also employ a wide variety of techniques. Clare Beaton's number book *One Moose, Twenty Mice* (Barefoot Books) uses felt applique embroidered with buttons, beads and ribbons. Bruce Ingham's unusual *A Night on the Tiles* (Methuen) uses splodges of paint and black and white stills from old movies while Sally Mavor uses three-dimensional models to make up the intriguing pictures for *The Hollyhock Wall* (Walker).

A SPRINGBOARD INTO ART

Apart from offering a wide range of visual experiences, picture books can also be an inspiration for your own art, craft and design activities. Many of the techniques used by picture book illustrators are simple and can be explored by the children. Show them Clare Beaton's felt applique illustrations before trying your own felt, bead and button collage. Use Eric Carle's paint and collage techniques as

the starting point for your own creations (see *The Very Hungry Caterpillar* 'Painted collage' page 50). Once you have introduced some of these techniques, encourage older children to look at the similarities between their artwork and the pictures in the book.

LEARNING TO READ PICTURES

Part of the child's visual education includes learning to interpret pictures. Just like written language, pictures have to be read - and children don't always read them in the way the artist intended, or in the way the adult or older child would interpret them. Invariably, these 'errors' stem from a lack of knowledge and experience rather than a lack of logic. For example, three-year-old Anna carefully studied a picture of a girl holding a large brown ball in front of her face, on the verge of throwing it in the air. With no personal experience of playing with large brown balls, she came up with her own interpretation and duly admired the huge Malteser the girl was about to eat! As she grows older, Anna will learn that such large Maltesers (sadly) do not exist. She will also learn to take note of the words to help her interpret the picture as the illustrator intended. In the meantime, given what she did and did not know about the world, her reading of the picture was perfectly logical.

You can do a lot to help the child make sense of pictures by looking out for and responding to queries and confusions. Some other typical questions include: *Where are the horse's legs?* (the horse is at the bottom of the page and we can only see his body); *Where is the man's face?* (the picture only shows the back of his head); *Where is Harry?* (the picture on the other page showed Harry, but Harry isn't in this picture.)

Sometimes, questions like these can be difficult to answer at a level appropriate for a young child. Don't worry too much about your response; although what you say can certainly help the child, the most important thing is plenty of experience. Gradually, she will come to accept that pictures don't show everything, and cease to be concerned by the gaps. Sniffing, stroking, even licking the page will eventually teach her that a picture only looks like an object - it doesn't necessarily smell or feel like it as well. She will also come to rely more and more on the words to help her make sense of the picture (as well as using the picture to help her make sense of the words.)

More specifically, the child has to learn about pictorial symbols in order to read pictures. When we look at the drawing of someone running, we know that the little lines are a cartoon shorthand for movement. We know what the speech bubble represents or that the small person at the top of the picture is meant to be in the distance. For the child, however, these symbols have to be learned, just as letters, sounds and letter clusters have to be learned. Again, the best way to help the child is through lots of exposure to different types of pictures - and some simple explanations when the child asks questions.

ROLE PLAY AND STORY TELLING

A good story makes one of the best starting points for role play. A strong beginning, a clearly delineated ending, appealing characters and a sequence of events gives the children a clear structure to follow. *Mr Gumpy's Outing* is a good example, as is Anita Hewitt's *Mrs Mopple's Washing Line* (Puffin) or Penny Dale's *Ten Play Hide and Seek* (Walker). You can also use role play to help the children explore

Creative Development

From: *Mr Gumpy's Outing*

whatever issues a particular story might raise.

A picture book can also be used as the inspiration for the child's own story telling. To begin with, a story can simply be retold in the child's own words. Older children can be asked to make up a different ending (see 'The ending', *Mr Gumpy's Outing*, page 37) or change one or two events in the story. With some books, you can lead the child off at a tangent so that the original story is simply a springboard into her own unique version (see 'Where will the balloon take you?', *The Blue Balloon*, page 43).

When encouraged to make up their own stories, even very young children will borrow language, characters and incidents from the stories they have heard. As well as exploring different aspects of story through role play, storytelling and art (see

Communication, Language and Literacy section 'Learning how a story works', page 12) you can help your children develop their story telling skills by sharing a wide range of different stories and repeating favourites as often as possible.

SINGING, MUSIC AND DANCE

Music is yet another creative way of exploring the themes, topics or ideas in a picture book. Books that feature animals or weather make particularly good starting points for playing percussion instruments and making up dance routines. Use the pictures and words in the book to introduce the nature and characteristics of whatever it is you want to explore through music (see *Dear Zoo*, 'Making a zoo', page 31).

A number of picture books take a

traditional song and illustrate it or use it as the basis for a new version. Jan Ormerod's *Ms McDonald Has a Class* (Red Fox) is loosely based on the original 'Old MacDonald' song whereas Colin and Jacqui Hawkins stick a little more closely to the originals in their *Old MacDonald had a Farm* and *I Know an Old Lady Who Swallowed a Fly* (Mammoth). Pippa Goodhart's *Row Your Boat* (Mammoth) is based on the well-known original song and comes complete with illustrations. Look out also for songs that link with the theme of a book. Sing 'Nellie the Elephant' to go with David McKee's *Elmer* books (Red Fox) or Winnie the Pooh's 'The More it Snows' song to go with Posy Simmonds' *F-Freezing ABC* (Red Fox).

See the 'Five-minute activities' in each book section for further suggestions of songs to match the theme of each picture book.

About Grandpa's Handkerchief

Grandpa's Handkerchief **is a delightful book with brightly coloured pictures and a friendly grandpa as the central character.**

The story takes us through Grandpa's week, showing us all the different things he can do with his collection of coloured handkerchiefs: *'On Monday, Grandpa used his yellow handkerchief for waving to trains. On Tuesday, Grandpa used his white handkerchief for bandaging a knee'* - and so on, through all the days of the week. The author, Dorothy Clark, uses both words and pictures to present the different colours. The picture clearly *shows* us the colour of the handkerchief while the words *tell* us the name of the colour. Each day of the week introduces a different colour, with a sports day and a holiday added on at the end.

The structure of the book itself is used to show how the week is made up. Just like the pages of a book, each day of the week is separate from the rest, yet follows on one after the other to create a *sequence*.

For a number of the activities linked with this book, you will need nine differently coloured handkerchiefs corresponding with those in the book. They are simple to make and provide a durable resource that can be used both in conjunction with the book and for other colour-related activities (see box below for instructions).

A C T I V I T Y - *Role play with handkerchiefs*

ABOUT THE ACTIVITY
Through role play, the children can explore and develop their understanding of the story. If you give them coloured handkerchiefs as a prop, the activity also helps colour recognition. Colour is a quality rather than an object. Because we cannot touch it or play with it, it is not always an easy concept for the child to grasp. One way of helping the child focus on colour, rather than the object, is to give her lots of things that are identical in every way except for their colour. Each handkerchief is the same size, shape and material, enabling the child to notice and focus on the one quality that is different - colour.

GROUP
Any size - adapt the number of characters to suit the number and age range in the group.

WHAT YOU WILL NEED
Grandpa's Handkerchief
Grandpa's handkerchiefs (see box)
Various other props (optional) - see below

WHAT TO DO
Once you have shared the book with the children a few times, read through the **Monday** page again. Look at the pictures and discuss what is happening. Invite the children to role play Monday's activity, using the yellow handkerchief. One approach is to choose a number of children to be the train and show them how to line up and hold onto the child in front. Give the driver a peaked cap and the guard a whistle or a bell. Depending on your group, give strict instructions as to where the train track runs. Make sure that the train goes past Grandpa a few times so that he can wave with his handkerchief and that the train returns to the station (you and the rest of the group).

◆ **Tuesday** - encourage the 'injured child' to think about how it feels when you hurt your knee and to act out her

How to make Grandpa's handkerchiefs
You will need 40cm squares of polycotton in appropriate colours - any good dressmaking shop or haberdashers should have a wide range at reasonable prices. Hem them with a sewing machine. If you choose fabric from a roll the smallest amount you can usually buy is .5m so you would have enough to make two hankies in each colour.

role. Encourage the group to think about what Grandpa might say when comforting the child. Be ready to help with tying the handkerchief around the knee.

◆ **Wednesday** - talk about pirates and the kinds of things they might do. Provide other handkerchiefs for pirate head-dresses (preferably white so that Grandpa's pink handkerchief stands out) and other props such as clip-on hoop earrings. If you can play this outside, use the climbing frame as the pirate ship.

Follow a similar approach for the remaining days. Some further suggestions for role-play props:

◆ **Thursday** - a pretend birthday cake, hats, balloons.

◆ **Friday** - a crumbly food for creating crumbs - cake, biscuit (real or pretend).

◆ **Saturday** - a stick to tie the handkerchief onto, for making a flag; a ball to play with (play outside if possible).

◆ **Sunday** - a spade; other gardening tools.

◆ **Holiday** - a boat, a stick for a mast (fold the handkerchief to make smaller if necessary). Put a lump of Plasticene into the boat to make it easier to attach the mast.

Grandpa's Handkerchief

◆ **Sports day** - a length of string with a FINISH sign attached.

The story, the props you provide and your input gives the children a format to work from. You may prefer not to provide any props at all, other than the coloured handkerchiefs. As much as possible, let the children develop the role play in their own way. Plan and prepare three or four handkerchiefs/days for each group activity - but be prepared to let one day's role play go on for the whole group session if the children are interested. While talking about each role play with the children, make lots of references to the relevant day and the colour of the handkerchief. This will help the children absorb the names of the weekdays and the colours.

MAKE A DISPLAY
At the end of the story on opening 15, we see Grandpa and the children pegging the handkerchiefs to a washing line. Rig up a washing line or string in your setting and peg on the handkerchiefs when you are not using them. Fold them in half or quarters if you are short of space. Write out the names of the colours to slip under the pegs so that the children can see and absorb names in print, along with the colours they represent.

ASSESSMENT
When assessing the child's performance in role play, always take into account previous experience, age, any special needs and whether English is the child's first language. Look out for how confidently the child performs, how accurately she has remembered the story and how she extends and develops her role. Does she express emotions? How imaginatively does she use facial expression and body language? Is she able to interact with other children?

EARLY LEARNING GOALS
Communication, Language and Literacy:
Listen with enjoyment, and respond to stories and make up their own stories.
Use language to imagine and recreate roles and experiences.
Creative Development:
Use their imagination in role play and stories.
Express and communicate their ideas, thoughts and feelings by using a widening range of materials, suitable tools, imaginative and role play.
Physical Development:
Move with confidence, imagination and in safety.

A C T I V I T Y - *Colour sorting with objects*

ABOUT THE ACTIVITY
This activity gives the child a hands-on opportunity to explore and learn to recognise different colours. It also gives the child experience of sorting objects through recognising colour similarities and differences.

For those children who are ready, the activity can be made more complex and challenging. A variety of carefully chosen objects enables the child to explore different shades and tones of the same colour.

GROUP
This activity can be adapted for any size group, but it is preferable to keep the group as small as possible.

WHAT YOU WILL NEED
A collection of familiar, everyday objects in the nine colour categories covered by the story - red, yellow, blue, green, orange, purple, white, pink and brown. If you wish, you can also add black objects. Store in a box or basket. Choose familiar and interesting things such as:
◆ building bricks of various types
◆ ribbons and buttons
◆ toothbrushes, flannels, soap

◆ toy vehicles, farm and jungle animals, dinosaurs
◆ teddies and other soft toys
◆ shells and pebbles
◆ coloured pencils, crayons and paintbrushes
◆ candles
◆ plastic cutlery, plates and cups

Try to include a range of shades and colour types within each group (pale blue, navy blue, sky blue, royal blue). Try also to have some objects which are identical but a different colour, such as a red toothbrush and a green toothbrush. Once you have gathered the objects, it is useful to keep them as a permanent resource, but you can also add perishable objects such as fruit, flowers, leaves, brown and white bread.

WHAT TO DO
Start off by showing the objects to the children and talking about them. Focus on elements such as the object's use, shape, texture and so on. Sort the objects in the basket onto Grandpa's handkerchiefs - all the blue objects on the blue handkerchief, all the red objects on the red handkerchief and so on. One way of organising the resources is to fold the handkerchiefs in half and place them in a semi-circle on

the floor so that they are easy to reach. Alternatively, the objects can be sorted into separate boxes. If you fold Grandpa's handkerchiefs and place them in the bottom of the boxes, this will help the children recognise where to place the objects.

Vary the number of objects you offer, depending on the developmental level and age of the group. With very little ones, stick to two or three colours and put just one object for each colour in the basket. This makes the activity a matching exercise - recognising the similar colour between the object and the handkerchief and putting them together. Gradually increase the number of colours and objects to sort. The challenge can be reduced by limiting the objects to a similar shade (all the darker blue objects, for example). The greatest challenge is provided by putting out all the objects so that the children have a wide range of colours and shades of colour to sort.

If you include objects which are similar but of a different colour, such as pencils, focus the child's attention on the fact that they are all pencils, but each one is a different colour. Try to include some objects whose colour is difficult to group, such as red/dark pink or dark sandy yellow/light brown. If the children realise that there is some question about an object's colour, discuss this with them and go along with their decision over where to put the object.

ASSESSMENT

Look out for signs that the child can recognise similarities and differences of colour and sort the objects accordingly. Can she organise her own work? Make a note of each child's ability to name the different colours, and the older child's ability to discriminate between different shades of colour.

EARLY LEARNING GOALS

Communication, Language and Literacy:
Interact with others, negotiating plans and activities and taking turns in conversation.
Knowledge and Understanding of the World:
Look closely at similarities, differences and change.
Creative Development:
Explore colour, texture, shape, form and space in two or three dimensions.

A C T I V I T Y - *Printing handkerchiefs*

ABOUT THE ACTIVITY

This activity helps children to explore and learn to recognise colour through making their own coloured handkerchiefs. It also introduces printing and colour-mixing techniques.

GROUP

Up to four children.

WHAT YOU WILL NEED

Grandpa's Handkerchief
Squares of white or pale coloured cotton, cut out with pinking shears - use an old sheet or shirts. Squares of light coloured paper could also be used - sugar paper works best for printing.

Circles of flat sponge soaked with undiluted, ready-mixed paint (dampen the sponge with water first so that the paint will soak in). Place in saucers or flat dishes.
A variety of objects to print with (see below).

Note: some objects (such as pieces of sponge) print better if dipped directly into a saucer of thick paint. Some (such as a string block) work better if painted with a brush. Experiment beforehand and provide the children with the appropriate materials.

WHAT TO DO

Tape or pin the squares of fabric to wooden boards or sugar paper to make them more stable to work on. Start off with just one or two colours. Provide a limited number of printing blocks or objects. Choose from:

◆ half a carrot
◆ half a potato with a handle cut into it to make it easy to hold
◆ a wooden block with string glued on, to make a textured pattern
◆ a cotton reel
◆ pieces of sponge
◆ dried beans or rice placed in a square of cotton and tied to make a bundle

Link the activity to *Grandpa's Handkerchief* by explaining that you are going to make your own coloured handkerchiefs. Show the child how to hold the object, cover it with paint and then press down firmly on the fabric. Demonstrate how to hold the fabric firm with the other hand before lifting off the object. Emphasise that the object needs to be kept still before lifting up, otherwise you get a smudged print.

Some objects are effective when used randomly, such as the sponge or the carrot. Others give a better result if spaced out

to show their distinctive patterns, such as the cotton reel or the string block. Draw lines or squares on the fabric with chalk and encourage children with sufficient hand control to use these guidelines to create a regular pattern. If you let the children do lots of try-outs on paper first, they will be able to experiment before doing their final version on the fabric.

Bear in mind that this activity is another means of exploring colour. Use the colour names as much as possible while you talk to the children about their printing. Extend the activity so that you have an example of each of the nine colours (try printing with white paint on coloured fabric). If you do not have ready-mixed paint in a range of colours, mix your own.

You can also show the children how to print one colour over another to create a new colour. Always print with the stronger colour first - blue before yellow, blue before red, red before yellow, red before white. Leave the first colour to dry. Encourage the children not to use too much of the first colour and plenty of the second.

MAKE A DISPLAY

When the handkerchiefs are dry they can be pegged onto the washing line along with their colour names. Compare them with Grandpa's handkerchiefs and discuss the similarities and differences. Use words such as plain and patterned, light, pale and dark.

ASSESSMENT

Do younger children understand the concept of printing? Look out for the point at which younger children start to print with the object rather than using it as a paintbrush. Observe the child's hand movements - can she keep the object still on the cloth or paper and hold down the cloth as she lifts the object up?

Are older children able to create patterns? Are they starting to show understanding that a pattern consists of a repeated motif or motifs? How successful are they in mixing colours and how creatively can they combine colours?

EARLY LEARNING GOALS

Creative Development:
Explore colour, texture, shape, form, and space in two or three dimensions.
Express and communicate their ideas, thoughts and feelings by using a widening range of materials, suitable tools ... designing and making.
Knowledge and Understanding of the World:
Look closely at similarities, differences, patterns and change.
Mathematical Development:
Talk about, recognise and recreate simple patterns.
Physical Development:
Handle tools, objects, construction and malleable materials safely and with increasing control.

FIVE-MINUTE ACTIVITIES

I CAN SING A RAINBOW

Suitable for a large group.
Have a group of eight children standing in the middle of the circle, each holding one of the handkerchiefs (the white is not needed). Start off with children who know the names of the colours. Ask them to listen carefully and wave their handkerchief when you and the rest of the children sing the name of the colour. Sing 'I Can Sing a Rainbow', slowing down when you sing the colour names. With younger ones or children who do not know the names, you or a helper can stand behind the children and help them to wave their handkerchief when the colour is sung (be prepared to work quickly so that the song doesn't drag).

COLOUR I SPY

Suitable for any size group.
Use the traditional format except that you are spying something of a given colour: 'I spy with my little eye something yellow like Grandpa's handkerchief.' Hold up Grandpa's handkerchief at the same time to help those children who have not yet learned the colour names. If necessary, you could direct the children to a particular part of the room: 'I spy with my little eye something yellow like Grandpa's handkerchief in the book corner.' Check that there are plenty of appropriately coloured objects visible in the room; plant some beforehand if necessary.

FIND GRANDPA'S HANDKERCHIEFS

A game for a group of four children. Draw squares on the playground using different coloured chalks. Limit the colours to three or four or use all nine, depending on the age and level of your group. Have more squares for each colour than the number of children. Hold up Grandpa's blue handkerchief and say *'It's Sunday. Grandpa needs his blue handkerchief.'* The children then have to find a blue square to stand in. If they do not know the colour names, they can look at the handkerchief you are holding and match its colour visually with the chalk square.
Increase the physical challenge by giving movement instructions: *'It's Sunday. Hop / jump / walk on tiptoes to Grandpa's blue handkerchief'.*

About Dear Zoo

First published in 1982, *Dear Zoo* was one of the first novelty books to achieve mass popularity. Compared with a lot of more recent novelty books, it is very simple - which is one of the many reasons why it works so well for young children.

The story is based on a request to the zoo for a pet. The zoo obligingly sends a succession of crates and boxes, each containing a possible pet. The crates and boxes are actually sturdy flaps so that the child can open the box to see what animal is inside. The text deliberately does not name the animals - *I wrote to the zoo to send me a pet. They sent me a ...* The child lifts the flap and there is an animal waiting to be recognised and identified. Each container matches the shape and size of the animal, so the giraffe's box is tall and thin; the snake's basket is round; the elephant's crate is huge. Many of the crates give a hint as to what might be inside: VERY HEAVY! says a message stamped on the elephant's crate, while the naughty monkey peeps out of the top of his box.

Once a crate is opened we are told why the pet is unsuitable. This gives the child a definitive characteristic to associate with each animal - the elephant is too *big*, the snake is too *scary*, the frog is too *jumpy*. In the end the zoo manages to send the perfect pet.

Like all the best picture books, *Dear Zoo* lends itself well to repeated readings. With each repetition, the child will become more and more able to participate by naming the animals and their characteristics.

ACTIVITY - *Animal flaps*

ABOUT THE ACTIVITY
This activity involves painting animals and making flaps to cover them. As well as matching shape and size, the children will need to investigate how the flaps in *Dear Zoo* are constructed, in order to create their own. The end result can then be played with in the same way.

GROUP
Any reasonable size for examining the flaps in *Dear Zoo*; no more than four or five children at a time for the art activity.

WHAT YOU WILL NEED
Dear Zoo
Sugar paper in different colours for the animals
Stiff card for the flaps
Paint
Printing materials such as sponge pieces and string blocks
Collage materials
Glue
Scissors
Large pieces of paper for the background

WHAT TO DO
Start off by looking at the flaps in *Dear Zoo*. Show the children the different ways in which they are joined to the page: the elephant's flap is stuck along the bottom edge so that you pull it down; the giraffe's flap is stuck along one side so that you open it like a door; the camel has two flaps, like double doors.

Prepare the art materials for the children. Depending on the age and developmental level of your children, you can either have pre-cut animal shapes for the children to decorate or templates for the children to draw around and cut out. If you have older children who are ready, encourage them to draw and cut out their own shapes. The shapes for the flaps can also be prepared in advance or made with the children. Use stiff card to ensure that the flaps are tough enough to withstand use, although the card does need to have some flexibility. Older ones may be able to place a sheet of card under an animal and draw a rectangle around the animal. They need to understand that the rectangle must cover the animal completely once it is cut out. If you plan to do this with the children, demonstrate to them first so that they can see the desired end result. Make sure that there is a large enough margin of card along the edge to stick on the flap.

Use whatever art techniques you wish to decorate the animals and their flaps. Make various options available to the children and help them to think about and choose colours and materials that suit the animals. Try some or all of the following:

◆ **Elephant:** make printing blocks by gluing lengths of string onto sanded chunks of wood. Print with black or dark grey paint onto lighter grey paper to make wrinkly skin. Stick on pieces of grey paper, felt or fabric.

◆ **Giraffe:** use yellow card or sugar paper and sponge print brown markings. Stick on strips of wool to make the tail and mane.

◆ **Lion:** stick on pieces of brown fur fabric to make the mane and tail.

◆ **Snake:** use printing techniques such as cut potatoes or cotton reels to create a repeating pattern along the body. Stick on small geometric shapes cut from shiny gold and silver paper. Colour in the body with layers of wax crayon and then engrave patterns into the wax with a pencil.

Dear Zoo

◆ **Frog:** use green and yellow chalk and smudge with a finger to colour the smooth body. Paint pieces of textured white wallpaper to make a bumpy back.

◆ **Birds:** use feathers (checking first for allergies) or torn strips of tissue paper. Birds such as parrots link with the zoo theme as well as being colourful.

◆ **Crates, boxes and baskets:** make a basket for the snake by gluing on pieces of straw to a yellow card background; make string blocks from lengths of string and print with brown paint onto brown card to make a wood grain pattern. Find wallpaper with a wood grain pattern or coloured textured paper.

Once you have finished your animals, glue them onto a background. Decide how you want your flap to open and make a fold along the appropriate edge of the flap shape. Glue on and leave to dry. If the glue isn't firm enough to withstand repeated opening, add a strip of clear tape. If the flaps do not stay shut, secure them with a blob of Blu-tack.

MAKE A DISPLAY

You can either make your animals into a frieze for the wall or a large book. Whichever you choose, make it accessible to the children so that they can lift the flaps and see which animal is inside each crate. Keep an eye on how they are being used and be ready to re-stick flaps or collage pieces.

Discuss with the children a heading for their book or frieze, such as: 'We have made our own Dear Zoo animals. Can you guess which animal is inside the box?'

Once the children have made their own flap pictures, make appropriate materials available so that they can explore this technique independently.

ASSESSMENT

Look out for signs that older children are fully exploring the flaps in *Dear Zoo*, and discovering how they work. Are they able to use size and shape discrimination to draw and cut out their own flaps? Look out for how safely and effectively the child handles the scissors, starting with her ability to hold them correctly. How well can she control a glue spatula or brush and is she able to use an appropriate amount of glue? How successfully can she print? (see Assessment for 'Printing handkerchiefs', page 28).

EARLY LEARNING GOALS
Mathematical Development:
Use language such as 'bigger' to describe the shape and size of solids and flat shapes.
Use everyday words to describe position.
Knowledge and Understanding of the World:
Look closely at similarities, differences, patterns and change. Ask questions about why things happen and how things work.
Physical Development:
Handle tools, objects, construction and malleable materials safely and with increasing control.
Creative Development:
Explore colour, texture, shape, form and space in two or three dimensions.
Express and communicate their ideas, thoughts and feelings by using a widening range of materials, suitable tools ... designing and making.

ACTIVITY- *Pets*

ABOUT THE ACTIVITY
Dear Zoo ends with the zoo finally sending a suitable pet in the form of a puppy. This can be used as the starting point for looking at pets, including the kinds of animals that make typical pets, their similarities and differences and how to look after them.

GROUP
Keep as small as possible when introducing the pets; up to six children for drawing and painting pets; one or two at a time for talking/writing about pet photographs.

WHAT YOU WILL NEED
Live pets brought in by their owners (check that the animal will react well to young children)
Pet accessories such as feeding bowls, leads, food, toys,
Paper, pencils and paint
Large table for display

WHAT TO DO
Look at the ending of *Dear Zoo* and talk about why the puppy makes a suitable pet as opposed to the zoo animals.

With the children, compile a list of all the different pets you can think of - cats, fish, budgies, rabbits, guinea pigs, gerbils, rats, mice, hamsters and so on.

Arrange for some pets to be brought into your setting. Establish how to handle the animal and whether or not the animal and owner are happy for the pet to be held or stroked. If there is any question of an animal not being comfortable with young children or any possible safety issues, do not allow the pet into the setting. Check that none of the children have allergies to animals. Have just a small group looking at the pet and, if possible, hold the group in a room away from the rest of the children so that the animal is not overwhelmed.

Ask the pets' owners to bring in any additional items such as feeding bowls, food, toys, bedding and brushes for grooming. Talk to the children about aspects of pet care that will make sense to them such as:
◆ feeding
◆ sleeping habits

◆ play and exercise
◆ cleaning
◆ health care
◆ discipline

The children will also love to hear any funny stories the owner may be able to tell them about his or her pet. Ask the owner if you can take photographs of the pet and its food, bedding, toys and so on.

MAKE A DISPLAY

Send a note home to parents asking for photographs of pets and any spare items to make up a 'Pets' corner' display. Add drawings and paintings of pets. You can also ask children to talk about their pet and write down their words to display alongside the photograph or drawing. Encourage the children to help you group the items in the display - all the cats and the cats' items together; all the small caged animals such as hamsters and gerbils together, and so on. Contact your local vet who may be able to let you have spare posters and information packs to add to your display.

ASSESSMENT

Observe how well the children can remember and follow instructions regarding the handling of pets brought into the setting. What previous knowledge, questions and thoughts does each child bring to the general discussion about pets?

How clearly can the child express herself when talking about photographs of her own pet and how well does she match what she says with the subject of the picture?

EARLY LEARNING GOALS

Communication, Language and Literacy:
Sustain attentive listening, responding to what they have heard by relevant comments, questions or actions. Extend their vocabulary.
Knowledge and Understanding of the World:
Find out about, and identify, some features of living things, objects and events they observe.
Personal, Social and Emotional Development:
Maintain attention, concentrate and sit quietly when appropriate.

A C T I V I T Y - *The zoo*

ABOUT THE ACTIVITY

Animals make up a broad category that can be grouped into a number of smaller categories. The 'Pets' activity above focuses on animals that fall into a particular group. This activity looks at animals that, in the UK, are only to be found in a zoo. If possible, the activity should follow on from a trip to a zoo.

GROUP

Any reasonable number for music and role-play activities; no more than four children at a time for craft activities.

WHAT YOU WILL NEED

Music activity: CD player or tape recorder with CDs or tapes to represent different zoo animals (see below for suggestions)
Role-play activity: card, scissors, paint, elastic or craft sticks for making masks (optional)
Craft activity: clay or playdough, penne pasta and matchsticks, paint, sponge pieces for printing, PVA glue, scrap materials (kitchen roll holders, boxes in different sizes, fabric, wool and felt scraps, drinking straws), twigs, green card for cutting out leaves, Plasticene, a large table for setting out the zoo, paper and pens for making notices.

WHAT TO DO

If possible, visit a zoo. Encourage the children to look out for certain animals - their appearance and their habitat. Try to take photographs of the animals you wish to focus on. If you are unable to visit a zoo, you may be able to get a video. Contact your nearest zoo and ask if they produce a video suitable for pre-school children or try your local library or educational resource centre.

Choose a limited number of animals to concentrate on, preferably those that made the biggest impact on the children and those that are featured in *Dear Zoo*. Prompt the children's memories with pictures, photographs and any information the zoo can let you have. You can then encourage the children to re-enact the zoo through music, role play and/or art.

◆ **Music:** Select pieces of music to represent different animals - something slow and lumbering for the elephant; something light and quick for the monkey. Try the following:

Elephant:	The Montagues and the Capulets from Prokofiev's *Romeo and Juliet*
Monkey:	Mercury from Holst's *Planet Suite*
Snake:	*Rhapsody in Blue*, George Gershwin
Lions and tigers:	*Night on a Bare Mountain*, Mussorgsky

Choose two pieces to play to the children and ask them to think about what zoo animal it reminds them of. Limit their choices to two animals if they need help with linking music to an idea or object: does *Rhapsody in Blue* make them think of a snake or an elephant? Encourage them to dance in time to the music, making appropriate movements for the animal: swinging arms to make a trunk, slow heavy stomping for an elephant; quick, light steps for a monkey.

Continue for as many different animals as you wish. If you can choose contrasting pieces of music and pairs of animals, it will help the children to make an appropriate link. Try elephant/monkey; lion/snake; tree frog/hippo.

Dear Zoo

If you have percussion instruments in your setting, you can also introduce the idea of representing animals with different percussion sounds - the drum for the elephant, the triangle for the monkey, the shakers for the snake. If your children are able to play the instruments fast/slowly and loudly/softly, encourage them to introduce these elements into their playing.

◆ **Role play:** Select a few animals that have characteristic and easy movements to act out such as the lumbering elephant, the slow stretching movements of the sloth, the waddling penguins. Practise these movements with the children. You can also role play feeding time at the zoo, drawing on your experiences if you were able to watch a zoo keeper feeding the animals. Choose feeding scenarios such as throwing fish to the seals, the monkeys and chimpanzees eating their fruit.

If you wish to introduce a craft element to the activity, cut out animal masks from card and paint them in appropriate colours. Attach thin elastic or glue onto a large craft stick so that the mask can be held in front of the face.

◆ **Making models:** Make your own zoo from playdough, clay or scrap materials - or a mixture of all three. Choose specific animals to concentrate on such as elephants, snakes, giraffes and monkeys. If you are using junk, pick animals that match the bits and pieces you have available. Try some of the following:

Elephants: Roll balls of clay or playdough. Pinch out big, flappy ears and attach a trunk. Alternatively, push a piece of penne pasta or a rolled-up length of grey card into the clay to make a trunk - the children may find this easier than joining a
separate clay piece to the main body. Paint spent matchsticks white and push them into the clay, one on each side of the trunk to make tusks. Attach short stumpy legs to the bottom of the elephant so that it can stand up. When the elephants have dried, glue on any bits that may have dropped off. Paint with thick grey paint and varnish with a mixture of PVA glue and water (approximately one part glue to three parts water).

Monkeys: Cut a kitchen roll holder into sections. Cut out pink circles and ask the children to draw on monkey faces. Paint the kitchen roll holders with thick brown paint. If you have brown fur fabric or felt pieces, these can be stuck on to create furry bodies. Cut out long curly tails from brown card, felt or fabric to glue onto the bottom of the kitchen roll.

Giraffes: Cover kitchen roll tubes, small and large boxes with thick yellow paint and sponge print with brown splodges to make the giraffe's neck, head and body. If the boxes are glossy you may need to paint and sponge print sugar paper and then cut out the pieces to glue to the sides of the boxes. Glue all the painted boxes together to make the giraffe. If you want to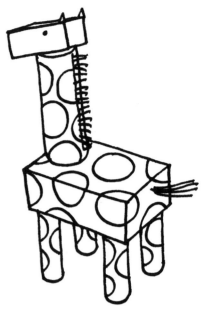
add legs, you can cut sections from a kitchen roll or make your own, thinner tubes from rolled card. You can also add a strip of fur fabric to the neck for a mane, and strips of wool to make a tail.

Snakes: Show the children how to roll a piece of clay or playdough between the hands to make a sausage. Put the sausage on the table and carry on rolling to make a snake. This takes quite a degree of hand control - be ready to help. Once the snake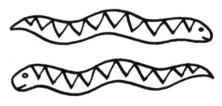
has been rolled, it can be decorated with dabs of coloured paint and varnished with a PVA glue solution.

Once you have made your animals, gather large boxes to make cages. Paint the boxes and cut out strips of card for bars, or attach white drinking straws with Blu-tack. Stick large twigs into Plasticene and attach cut-out green leaves to make vegetation. Wedge some of the monkeys in the trees or hang them from their tails. Use an old plastic fish tank for your snakes. Sprinkle sand and gravel in the bottom and put in some vegetation. Make trees from rolled-up brown sugar paper and cut out green leaves for your giraffes to nibble. Glue straw and sand to sheets of green paper for the giraffes and elephants to stand on. Add some pebbles and stones. Set out the different habitats on a large table. Involve the children as much as possible in making the habitats and arranging the animals. Sit down with the children and plan the signs and notices for the zoo, making a note of their suggestions on your clip-board. You could include signs such as 'Do not feed the monkeys' and notices giving some basic information about each group of animal, tailored to your age group. For example, where the animal comes from, what it eats. The children can also think up names for their animals.

ASSESSMENT

Music activities: look out for how well the child can dance in time to the music and express different animal characteristics and behaviours through movement. If you use percussion instruments, make a note of whether younger children can hold them correctly and produce sound from them. Can older children make loud/soft sounds and play a rhythm slowly and quickly?

Role play: see Assessment for 'Grandpa's Handkerchief role play', page 25.

Making models: look out for how well the children can balance and join the separate parts to make giraffes and monkeys. Are they able to control and manipulate the clay to model elephants and snakes? See 'Animal flaps' page 29 for assessment of cutting, gluing and printing skills.

EARLY LEARNING GOALS
Music activity:

Creative Development:
Recognise and explore how sounds can be changed, sing simple songs from memory, recognise repeated sounds and sound patterns and match movements to music.
Physical Development:
Move with confidence, imagination and in safety.

Role play:

Communication, Language and Literacy:
Listen with enjoyment, respond to stories, and make up their own stories.
Use language to imagine and recreate roles and experiences.
Physical Development:
Move with confidence, imagination and in safety.

Making models:
Creative Development:
Explore colour, texture, shape, form and space in two or three dimensions.
Knowledge and Understanding of the World:
Build and construct with a wide range of objects, selecting appropriate resources, and adapting their work where necessary.
Select the tools and techniques they need to shape, assemble and join materials they are using.

Physical Development: Handle tools, objects, construction and malleable materials safely and with increasing control.

For all three activities:
Creative Development:
Express and communicate their ideas, thoughts and feelings by using a widening range of materials, suitable tools, imaginative and role play ... movement ... songs and musical instruments.
Use their imagination in art and design, music, dance, imaginative and role play and stories.
Knowledge and Understanding of the World:
Find out about, and identify, some features of living things, objects and events they observe.
Observe, find out about and identify features in the place they live and the natural world.
Find out about their environment, and talk about those features they like and dislike.

FIVE-MINUTE ACTIVITIES

WHICH ANIMAL?

Play a listening game based on role playing the animals in *Dear Zoo*. Play music for the children to dance to. When the music stops, the children have to listen to the animal you name and then be that animal. Choose some characteristic movements - jumping up and down for a monkey, wriggling on the floor for a snake, frog leaps, swinging your arm like an elephant's trunk.

Vary your instructions by whispering the animal, or holding up a picture. If you play this with a small group of older children who are starting to

read, you could also hold up the name of the animal.

WHAT'S BEHIND THE FLAP?

Gather different animals from the *Dear Zoo* story. Glue a triangle of stiff card to the back of a large piece of card so that it stands up by itself, or fold a piece of card in half. Place it on the table to make a flap and then hide an animal behind it. Explain to the children that you want them to guess what zoo animal is behind the flap and that you are going to give them some clues.

Start off by making the clues general, such as 'This animal is very big' or 'This animal is about the same size as the shed in the garden'. You can then be more specific - 'This animal is grey', ending up with a give-away - 'This animal has big ears, two tusks and a long trunk'. Tailor the language you use to the age and developmental level of your group.

About Mr Gumpy's Outing

John Burningham is one of the best picture book authors/illustrators around - and *Mr Gumpy's Outing* is probably his best loved book.

The story is based on the traditional sequence format with lots of repetition. One by one, Mr Gumpy gathers a collection of unruly children and animals for a trip in his boat. Despite his warnings, they all misbehave, with the kind of predictable and dramatic results that young children love.

The story and pictures introduce the themes of number and sequence. The left-hand pages have small, monochrome drawings which show the number of passengers in the boat increasing one by one, from one (Mr Gumpy) to ten (Mr Gumpy, the children, the rabbit, the cat and so on.) The right-hand pages introduce each new passenger in a large and beautiful, coloured picture. Together, the pages clearly demonstrate that the sequence is built up by the addition of one new animal each time.

Mr Gumpy's Outing can be used as the starting point for a number of other themes and topics, including water and animals.

A C T I V I T Y - *Making animal props*

ABOUT THE ACTIVITY

This is a craft activity that can be linked with the role-play activity (see page 35). While it is not essential for the children to make their own props, it adds to the fun if they can dress up in animal costumes they have made themselves. Apart from using cutting and sticking skills, the activity encourages the children to look at characteristic animal features. For example, the curly tail and distinctive shape of a pig's snout; the woolly coat of the sheep; the colour and shape of a cockerel's coxcomb.

GROUP

Up to four children at a time.

WHAT YOU WILL NEED

Mr Gumpy's Outing
Pictures of the various animals in the story
Plastic hair bands (ask parents to donate spare ones)
Old ties and/or belts
Stiff card and marker pen
Ear and tail templates, pencils and scissors for children who are ready to draw around and cut out shapes independently
Paint in appropriate colours for the different animals (such as pink, white, brown, grey)
Sponge pieces for printing
Fabric scraps/cotton wool/tissue paper
Glue
Toilet rolls

WHAT TO DO

Before making a set of props, look at the large picture of the animal in *Mr Gumpy's Outing* and discuss the ears, tail and any other feature you want to create. Provide more pictures of each animal so that the child can see that all rabbits have long ears, short furry tails and so on. Talk about the children's pets where relevant. Introduce appropriate describing words - *long, thin* ears for the rabbit, *curly* tail for the pig.

If the child is to use these props in her role play, they need to be tough. Use stiff card for the ears and tails. Make sure the card is firm enough to stand upright without flopping over, but not too stiff to cut out. The props also need to be wearable. Ears, horns and coxcombs can be glued to a plastic head-band. Cut out a double pair of ears and glue around the band (see illustration). Tails need to be attached to a belt or tie that can be worn around the waist. Punch a hole in the end of the tail and tie it onto the belt with a piece of string (see illustration). Use the strongest card you can find and keep the longer tails as short and as wide as possible, to prevent them getting torn during the role play.

Depending on how much your group can do for themselves, you can provide ready-cut ears and tails, or pre-drawn shapes for them to cut out, or you can give them templates. As with any craft activity, encourage the children to do as much for themselves as possible.

Decorate ears and tails with sponge printing or by gluing on scraps of felt or fake fur fabric. A combination of both printing and collage is effective. Encourage the children to explore different colours and materials and to choose what *they* think is most appropriate for the different animals. The following suggestions can be used as a starting point:

◆ **Rabbit:** make the rabbit's tail by gluing cotton-wool balls onto a disc of card. Cotton wool can also be used for ears.

◆ **Pig:** make the pig's snout by cutting a section from a toilet roll and gluing a circle of card over one end. Paint with thick pink paint and add two spots of black paint or felt pen for nostrils. This can then be threaded onto elastic and worn around the head over the child's nose. Bear in mind that some children may not be comfortable about wearing the snout. To make the curly tail, cut out a circle of pink card and draw a spiral in felt pen. Sponge print the circle and then cut around the spiral.

◆ **Sheep:** use cotton-wool balls or natural coloured wool to glue onto the sheep's ears and tail. If you live in the country, gather real sheep's wool. Wash it in detergent before giving it to the children.

◆ **Chicken:** cut out a row of triangles from stiff card. Decorate with pieces of bright red tissue paper or shiny paper. These can then be attached to the plastic head-band. Tail feathers can also be cut out from card and decorated with strips of red, orange and yellow tissue. Try tearing the strips to get a feathery effect. If you have a source of real feathers, these can also be glued onto the tail (check first that no child has an allergy to feathers).

◆ **Calf and goat:** horns can be cut from card or made from rolled-up paper and attached to the head-band along with or instead of ears. When looking at the pictures, draw the children's attention to the differences between the goat's and the calf's horns.

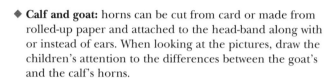

To make enough props for all the animals in the story and the children in your group, you will need to hold several sessions. If the props are to be used in the role play, it is important that they are robust. Check the children's work after the session has ended. Re-glue any part that is looking a bit loose and make sure the ears and tails are as firmly attached as possible.

ASSESSMENT
Observe how the child handles scissors and glue (see Assessment for 'Animal flaps' page 30).
Can the older child choose appropriate techniques and materials for the particular animal features she is making?

EARLY LEARNING GOALS
Physical Development:
Handle tools, objects, construction and malleable materials safely and with increasing control.
Creative Development:
Explore colour, texture, shape, form and space in two or three dimensions.
Express and communicate their ideas, thoughts and feelings by using a widening range of materials, suitable tools ... designing and making.
Knowledge and Understanding of the World:
Find out about, and identify, some features of living things, objects and events they observe.
Build and construct with a wide range of objects, selecting appropriate resources, and adapting their work where necessary.
Select the tools and techniques they need to shape, assemble and join materials they are using.

ACTIVITY - *Role play*

ABOUT THE ACTIVITY
The simple but orderly structure of the story makes it ideal for role playing. The children gain an active experience of the number sequence as they climb into the boat one by one. The nub of the story is a 'cause and effect': *'The goat kicked / The calf trampled / The chickens flapped .... The rabbit hopped / The children squabbled / The boat tipped ....'* turn over the page *'and into the water they fell.'* If the children themselves squash into the boat one by one until it is full, and then tip out with a 'splash', it gives them experience of concepts such as 'cause and effect' and 'full' and 'empty'.

The characters in the story are particularly suitable for role play by young children. Each animal has its own special behaviour - the children squabble, the rabbit hops, the cat chases the rabbit, the sheep bleats, the chicken flaps, and so on. This gives the children clear actions and noises to perform.

GROUP
Adapt the number of characters to suit any size group or age range.

WHAT YOU WILL NEED
Mr Gumpy's Outing
Animal props made by the children
A hat and a pole for Mr Gumpy
Clothes for the children, such as a cap and a sun hat or large T-shirts
A boat, such as a group of small chairs or cushions arranged in a boat shape

WHAT TO DO
This activity can be introduced once you have shared *Mr Gumpy's Outing* with the children a few times.
Set up the boat and have ready the animal props and clothes for Mr Gumpy and the children.

Mr Gumpy's Outing

Read through the story again and encourage the children to perform the different noises and actions. Explain and demonstrate any words that may be unfamiliar, such as trample, bleat or squabble. Link with their own experiences as much as possible - What do they say and do when they squabble with their brothers and sisters? Has any child got a cat and a dog? How does the dog tease the cat? You could use the 'Mr Gumpy had a boat' song (see page 38) as a preparation for the role play.

Assign roles to the children and help them to put on their ears and tails. Show them how to sit on their chairs so that they do not squash their tails. Position Mr Gumpy by the boat with his pole. Encourage each animal to come up, one at a time, to ask for a ride before getting into the boat. If necessary, remind the animals and Mr Gumpy of the words they use: '*Can I come along, Mr Gumpy?*' '*Yes .... if you don't squabble.*'

In the story, the animals squabble, hop and trample all at the same time. Depending on the size of your group, you may find it works better for each animal to perform its action one at a time before falling into the water with a splash! Mr Gumpy has ten types of animal in his boat by the time he sets out, but you may find the group easier to manage if you limit the number. Choose roles carefully - it is preferable for the kicking goat to be one of the calmer children, for example.

After the animals have fallen into the water with a splash, encourage them to climb out onto the bank to walk to Mr Gumpy's house for tea. As this is quite an active role play, make the most of the ending to settle any children who

have become over-excited. Finish off quietly with everybody sitting down for tea. Mr Gumpy can then wave goodbye to all the animals as they walk back to their seats.

The story gives the children a structure to follow but, as with any role play, allow the children the freedom to develop it in their own way.

ASSESSMENT
See Assessment for 'Grandpa's Handkerchief role play', page 26.

EARLY LEARNING GOALS
Communication, Language and Literacy:
Listen with enjoyment, and respond to stories ... and make up their own stories.
Use language to imagine and recreate roles and experiences.
Creative Development:
Use their imagination in role play and stories.
Express and communicate their ideas, thoughts and feelings by using a widening range of materials, suitable tools, imaginative and role play.
Knowledge and Understanding of the World:
Find out about, and identify, some features of living things, objects and events they observe.
Observe, find out about and identify features in the place they live and the natural world.
Find out about their environment, and talk about those features they like and dislike.
Physical Development:
Move with confidence, imagination and in safety.

ACTIVITY - *Sink and float*

ABOUT THE ACTIVITY
In *Mr Gumpy's Outing*, the story centres around everyone falling into the water with a splash. This can be used as a starting point for a sink and float activity, enabling the children to observe and explore objects sinking or floating in water. The activity encourages scientific skills such as observing, testing and predicting. It also gives the children a technique for recording their results.

GROUP
Up to four children.

WHAT YOU WILL NEED
Mr Gumpy's Outing
A large bowl of water - preferably clear plastic
A collection of everyday objects (see below)
Two plastic mats
Two plastic hoops or plastic boxes
A label saying 'sink' and a label saying 'float'
A towel for drying hands

WHAT TO DO
Prepare your resources: a large bowl of water on a waterproof mat, a collection of objects, a second mat with either two hoops or two plastic boxes, one labelled 'sink' and the other 'float'. Choose a variety of objects that will sink and a variety that will float. Include some that are buoyant, such as a cork and a ping-pong ball, and some which will sink immediately, such as a stone and a key. Include others that will sink more slowly, such as a shell.

Look at the relevant pages of *Mr Gumpy's Outing* - the boat floating in the water on opening 13 and the passengers falling into the water on opening 14. Talk about how the boat is *floating* on the water and how the animals fall into the water but do not *sink* - they manage to swim to the bank and climb out. Show the children the small monochrome drawing of everybody safely on the bank on opening 15.

Introduce the bowl and the objects. Explain that you are going to be scientists and do an experiment to find out if objects sink or float in the water. Choose an object and place it slowly and carefully on the water. Watch to see whether it sinks or floats. Fish it out of the water and place it in the relevant box or hoop. Invite a child to come and choose an object to try. Show her where to place the object once it has been tested. Continue until all the objects have been tested and sorted. Once the children understand the process, encourage them to continue independently in small groups, finding objects to test and placing them in the appropriate box. They can also be asked to predict whether an object will sink or float before testing.

MAKE A DISPLAY

Explain to the children that scientists must record what happened when they have finished their experiment. Discuss with them possible ways of recording - for example, drawing pictures of the tested objects and gluing them onto two differently coloured sheets of paper with the headings 'sink' and 'float'. As always, involve the children in the cutting, arranging and sticking. Have ready a clip-board with paper and marker pen and ask the children to decide what you should write as an explanation of the activity. Their explanation can then be turned into a heading for the display. The pictures of the objects can also be labelled. If you have any writers in your group, they can write or copy the name of the object, to be stuck beside its picture.

ASSESSMENT

Look out for how closely the child observes what is happening. How accurately can older children predict what is likely to happen? Are they able to carry out the activity independently? How appropriate are the objects that the older child chooses to test for herself? Encourage the older child to organise her own recording as much as possible. This will help you assess the degree to which the child understands the process and purpose of recording, as well as the activity itself.

EARLY LEARNING GOALS

Knowledge and Understanding of the World:
Investigate objects and materials by using all of their senses as appropriate.
Observe, find out about and identify features in the place they live and the natural world.

Communication, Language and Literacy:
Interact with others, negotiating plans and activities and taking turns in conversation.
Extend their vocabulary.

Physical Development:
Handle tools, objects, construction and malleable materials safely and with increasing control.
Use a range of small and large equipment.

ACTIVITY - The ending

ABOUT THE ACTIVITY

It is important for the child to discover that stories have endings. Finding out 'what happens in the end' is what keeps us going until we have finished the book. Good endings can also be important for young children in terms of leaving them feeling safe and comfortable. *Mr Gumpy's Outing* is a safe story with a sound ending. Although everyone behaves badly and they all fall into the water, Mr Gumpy (unlike the chickens) does not flap. He even takes everybody back to his house for tea and invites them for a ride another day. The ending is emphasised by Mr Gumpy saying goodbye to everyone against a night sky - the end of the day as well as the end of the story.

Focusing on the ending and thinking of different endings can highlight this aspect of the story.

GROUP

Up to six children.

WHAT YOU WILL NEED

Mr Gumpy's Outing
Clip-board, paper and marker pen
Paper for drawing or painting, paints and/or crayons

WHAT TO DO

Look at the ending of *Mr Gumpy's Outing*, taking it from the point where everybody goes back to Mr Gumpy's house for tea. Discuss the ending with the children. Highlight elements with a particular link to endings, such as Mr Gumpy saying goodbye to everybody and inviting them to come for a ride on another day. Point out to the children that Mr Gumpy is waving goodbye and that it is night time. Compare the dark sky with the sky in earlier pictures.

Mr Gumpy's Outing

Ask the children if they can remember what the animals did in the story when they climbed onto the bank. Explain that you are going to think of some different things for them to do. Ask a child with good verbal skills to tell the group what he or she thinks the animals did after climbing out onto the bank. Alternatively, start the children off with some ideas of your own.

As this is an ending, the child's alternative suggestion should not go on for too long. Finish off each suggestion with Mr Gumpy saying goodbye and waving to the animals, to emphasise that this is the ending of the story. Write down each child's endings, keeping to their own words as much as possible. Explain that you have written down what Ali has said and that you are going to read his words to the group. You can also try role playing the different endings. Some children may simply re-tell the original ending or change only one or two points. Leave each child to respond at his or her own level of readiness. Even if the child simply retells the ending, she is still gaining a valuable language experience as well as the chance to focus on the ending.

MAKE A DISPLAY
Turn the endings into a group book. Write out the different endings, ensuring that each one finishes with Mr Gumpy saying and waving goodbye. Ask the children to draw or paint a picture of their ending. Make a simple book by punching holes in the top left-hand corner of thin card and tying the sheets with a ribbon. Stick the words and pictures onto the pages, one ending for each page. Head each page with the child's name: 'Hannah's ending'; 'Deepak's ending'. Discuss with the children an explanation for the cover of the book, such as: 'We have thought of some new endings for *Mr Gumpy's Outing*'.

Involve any children who are ready with as much of the writing as they can manage, as well as cutting and sticking. Read through your book with the children and hang it from a hook in the book corner.

ASSESSMENT
Use the content of the child's made-up ending as a means of assessing how well she understands the concept. Is she able to finish off her story or does she need prompting from the adult? To what degree does her ending link with the original story? How fluently and confidently does she express herself and how wide is her vocabulary?

EARLY LEARNING GOALS
Communication, Language and Literacy:
Enjoy listening to and using spoken and written language, and readily turn to it in their play and learning.
Sustain attentive listening, responding to what they have heard by relevant comments, questions or actions.
Speak clearly and audibly with confidence and control and show awareness of the listener.
Listen with enjoyment, respond to stories and make up their own stories.
Use language to imagine and recreate roles and experiences.
Retell narratives in the correct sequence, drawing on language patterns of stories.
Show an understanding of the elements of stories, such as main character, sequence of events, and openings.
Creative Development:
Use their imagination in role play and stories.
Personal, Social and Emotional Development:
Maintain attention, concentrate and sit quietly when appropriate.

FIVE-MINUTE ACTIVITIES

MR GUMPY HAD A BOAT

Sing 'Mr Gumpy had a boat/Ee-aye ee-aye oh' to the tune of 'Old MacDonald'. Use the animals in the story and the noises or actions they make. Go through the animals beforehand, practising the noises and actions. Encourage the children to perform the actions as you sing.

MR GUMPY'S ANIMALS

Play a listening game. Go through the animals and their noises or actions. Choose clear actions for squabbling or teasing, such as shaking a finger or making tickling movements with the hands. Play music for the children to dance to, and when the music stops, name an animal. They then have to remember and perform the action or sound. If necessary, limit the number of animals you use. Explain to the children that when the music starts again, it is time for them to finish their action and dance. This helps you to manage what can be a lively group activity.

PLASTICENE BOATS

Give the children a short introduction to the different shapes that float. Have a ball of Plasticene and a bowl of water. Drop the Plasticene into the water and watch it sink. Fish out the Plasticene and fashion it into a boat shape. Place gently into the water and observe it floating. Depending on the attention span of your children, go through stages in flattening the Plasticene. Let the children explore with the Plasticene, softening it in warm water first so that it is easier to manipulate.

About The Blue Balloon

The Blue Balloon is a delightful and unusual picture book with surprise after surprise hidden inside its pages. A little boy finds a soggy old balloon in the garden. In the tradition of all good stories, the balloon turns out to be rather more than it first appears - with all kinds of strange and unexpected results.

A magical balloon which can change its shape, size, colour and behaviour provides a good vehicle for introducing a range of different concepts. The story also includes an imaginary adventure when the balloon takes off into space, as well as action words when the boy tries bursting the balloon by squeezing, squashing, wacking and running it over.

Throughout the book, the little boy is accompanied by his dog, Kipper. Some children may recognise Kipper from other Mick Inkpen stories. The pictures show Kipper's humorous reactions to the boy's antics with the balloon, although like the fox in *Rosie's Walk*, he is never mentioned in the text.

Mick Inkpen's illustrations are worth a special mention. At first glance, he appears to be just another cartoon illustrator. A closer look reveals beautiful misty watercolours and a particularly delicate quality to his line. The blue balloon gleams against the white background and the sausage-shaped rainbow-coloured balloon at the end of the book is particularly beautiful.

A C T I V I T Y - *Exploring balloons*

ABOUT THE ACTIVITY
The blue balloon in the story occasionally behaves like a normal balloon. This makes a good starting point for a series of experiments designed to explore balloons and their qualities. As part of the activity, the children can be encouraged to predict, observe, compare, describe results and record - all of which are important scientific skills. In describing what happens to the balloons, you can also introduce a number of new words.

GROUP
Up to six children.

WHAT YOU WILL NEED
The Blue Balloon
A number of good quality balloons. Check that they are easy to blow up.
String
A marker pen
Thick paint
Paper and drawing pencils for recording
Long strips of backing paper for display
Clip-board/paper

WHAT TO DO
◆ **BLOWING UP BALLOONS** - Choose one of the balloons and explain that you are going to blow it up. Ask the children to predict what will happen when you start to blow into the balloon. Keep stopping, as you blow, to look at how the balloon's size increases each time. Use language such as 'bigger' and 'fatter'.

Tie string to the end of the balloon and then compare the blown-up balloon with a deflated balloon of the same shape and colour. How are the shape and size different? How is the colour different? Let the children feel the two balloons and compare them.

Blow up another balloon and hold the end tightly to keep in the air. Ask the children to predict what will happen when you let go. Show the children the picture on opening 7 of *The Blue Balloon*, where the boy lets go of the balloon.

If any children would like a turn, blow it up for them and pass it to them, showing them how to squeeze the end tightly before letting go.

Bear in mind that balloons are unpredictable when the air is suddenly released. Some children may be unnerved by this. The activity can also cause great excitement. Your group will be easier to manage if you can limit the number of excitable children at any one time, and keep it as small as possible. It is also less distracting to others in the room if you can do this outside.

With older children, you can start to talk about what is happening to the balloon. Blowing in air makes the rubber stretch so that the balloon grows bigger. Get the children to breathe in so that they can feel the air going into their lungs. Help them to discover the effects of blowing by asking them to blow onto their hands. What can they feel? Give them a feather or a piece of tissue to blow at so they can observe the power of blowing out air. Keep a careful eye on the group - if children breathe in and blow out too enthusiastically, they could make themselves dizzy.

MAKE A DISPLAY
Put out a deflated balloon and a fully blown balloon for the children to look at and draw. Help them to create a series of drawings for the 'in-between' stages, showing each balloon a little bigger than the last. Cut out the drawings, put them in order and stick them onto a long strip of paper as a record of what happens when the balloon is blown up. Involve the children with the cutting, sticking and ordering as much as

possible. Plan with the children an explanation of the experiment to write out as a heading, such as 'When we blow air into the balloon it gets bigger and bigger and bigger. We tie a knot in the end to keep the air in the balloon.' This can be added to the drawings and put up on the wall. You can also attach balloons in all the stages of being blown up to a long strip of paper.

◆ **BIGGER AND BIGGER** - Ask a child to draw on a balloon with a strongly coloured, thick felt-pen. Ask the children to predict what will happen to the drawing when you blow up the balloon.

Stop and look at the picture after each blow. Make another drawing on a second balloon and compare the two pictures. Look at how the felt-pen line stretches and becomes fainter.

MAKE A DISPLAY
Ask three children to draw a similar shape or pattern on three balloons. Plan with the children an explanation of the activity to write out for display, such as 'When we blow air into the balloon, the drawing gets bigger and bigger.' Leave one balloon as it is, blow one half full of air and the third completely full of air. Attach the balloons in order to a long strip of paper, add the heading and display on the wall.

◆ **PAINTING BALLOONS** - Show the children how to put thick blobs of paint on a balloon before it is blown up. Leave them to dry. Ask the children to predict what will happen when the balloon is blown up. Stop to look after each blow. Help the children to describe what has happened to the paint, introducing language such as 'cracked'.

MAKE A DISPLAY
Ask the children to record their work for display by decorating a number of balloons with thick paint. Keep half as they are and blow up the other half, once the paint is dry. Plan an explanation such as 'When we blow up our balloons the paint stretches and cracks.' Attach the deflated balloons to one side of a strip of paper and the bunch of blown-up balloons on the other side. Write out the explanation and stick it in between the two bunches.

◆ **STICKY BALLOONS** - Look at opening 5 of *The Blue Balloon*, where the little boy rubs the balloon and sticks it to the ceiling. Show the children how to rub a blown-up balloon against a jumper or hair so that it will stick to the wall. Explain to older children that rubbing the balloon creates static electricity and this is what makes the balloon stick to the wall.

MAKE A DISPLAY
Ask the children to draw pictures of rubbing the balloon against a jumper and the balloon stuck to the wall. Discuss explanations of the experiment to write out and add to the drawings. Display on the wall.

◆ **FLOAT AND SINK** - Prepare a large bowl of water and blow up a balloon. Ask a child to place the balloon on the water. Ask the children to describe what has happened. Introduce the word 'float' if necessary. Pour water into a second balloon, either from the tap or a large jug. Tie the end of the balloon. Give the children the opportunity to hold and feel the water-filled balloon. Ask them to predict what will happen when the balloon is put in the water. Ask a child to do so and discuss what happens, introducing the word 'sink', if necessary. With older ones, talk about the air in the balloon making it light so that it floats on water, and the water in the balloon making it heavy so that it sinks.

MAKE A DISPLAY
Ask the children to draw pictures of one balloon sinking and one balloon floating. Discuss an explanation to write up and stick with the pictures. Alternatively, put out two bowls of water with the two balloons. Impress upon the children that the display is delicate and must be treated with care.

ASSESSMENT
Look out for how closely the child observes what is happening and whether the older child can predict what is likely to happen. Can the child follow instructions and carry out the activities independently? Encourage the older child to organise her own recording as much as possible. This will help you assess the degree to which the child understands the process and purpose of recording as well as the activities themselves.

EARLY LEARNING GOALS
Knowledge and Understanding of the World:
Investigate objects and materials by using all of their senses as appropriate.
Look closely at similarities, differences, pattern and change.
Ask questions about why things happen and how things work.
Communication, Language and Literacy:
Interact with others, negotiating plans and activities and taking turns in conversation.
Extend their vocabulary.
Physical Development:
Handle tools, objects, construction and malleable materials safely and with increasing control.
Use a range of small and large equipment.

A C T I V I T Y - *S h a p e s,   s i z e s   a n d   c o l o u r s*

ABOUT THE ACTIVITY

The blue balloon has a tendency to change its shape, size and colour. Wherever possible, the pages themselves reflect these changes. For instance, when the balloon grows huge, it is given a page that can be unfolded to poster size. When Kipper and the boy stretch the balloon, a section of the page unfolds to accommodate both the balloon and the word: 'stre-e-e-e-e-e-e-e-e-e-e-e-e-e-e-ee-e-e-e-e-e-etched'. Clever little touches such as these make the story a delight for both adults and children.

The book provides an original starting point for looking at colour, shape and size. These activities focus on different shapes, sizes and colours through making lots of different balloons. The children will use cutting, sticking and drawing skills.

GROUP

Up to four children.

WHAT YOU WILL NEED

The Blue Balloon
A selection of different coloured balloons
A selection of different shaped balloons
Coloured sugar paper
Various templates (optional)
Scissors, glue, pencil
White paint and brush
Thick paint and sponges for printing
Backing paper
Clip-board and marker pen

WHAT TO DO

◆ **COLOUR** - Gather a selection of different coloured balloons to show the children. See how many colours they can name. Play a matching game, where you give a child a balloon and ask her to choose another one of the same colour. Put strings on to the balloons so they are easy to hold and have the two sets of balloons tied to the back of a sturdy chair, a rack for drying paintings or an upturned laundry basket. Make sure a helper is on hand to help the children tie and untie the balloons.

Show the children the rainbow-coloured balloon on opening 15 and explain to them that you are all going to make your own different coloured balloons.

You can either give the children ready-cut balloons in different coloured sugar paper so that this is a colour recognition and sticking activity, or you can give them templates to draw around and cut out, to make a cutting and sticking activity. Best of all, encourage them to draw their own balloons free hand.

Show the children the blue balloon on the cover of the book and point out the patch of white. Show the children how to paint a splodge of white onto their balloons, near the top and slightly to one side.

MAKE A DISPLAY

Stick the balloons on to large sheets of paper in their colour groups. Cut out small triangles to represent the knot at the end of the balloon and show the children how to glue on the triangles with a length of string.

Discuss an explanation of the display with the children and make a note of their suggestions on your clip-board. Write out your heading along with the names of the different colours to glue beside each colour group.

◆ **SHAPE** - Look at the picture on opening 10, where the balloon disappears and then reappears as a square shape. If possible, find some balloons in different shapes and show them to the children.

Give the children ready-cut shapes from sugar paper, or shape templates to draw around and cut out. Older ones may be able to draw some shapes themselves. Explain to the children that you are going to make your own magic balloons in different shapes - not just square ones.

Use the shape names as much as possible - circle, square, triangle, hexagon, rectangle, rhombus. Decorate your balloons with sponge printing. Show the children how to put a blob of white paint on the corner of the balloon.

If you wish, you could extend beyond geometric shapes and create leaf-shaped balloons, cloud-shaped balloons, car-shaped balloons, and so on. Give the children templates or encourage them to draw their own.

MAKE A DISPLAY

Plan a heading with the children, write out the names for the different shapes and stick them to backing paper along with string and a little triangle for each balloon.

The Blue Balloon

◆ **SIZE** - Look at the huge balloon on opening 7 and the small balloon once the air is let out. Look at the long thin balloon on opening 8 when it is stretched. Look at the long fat balloon on opening 15.

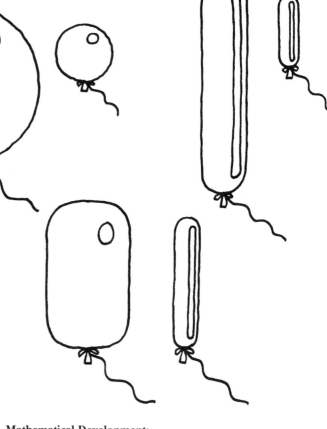

Draw different sized balloons with the children - big balloons and small balloons; huge balloons and tiny balloons; long balloons and short balloons; thin balloons and fat balloons. Add blobs of white paint to round balloons and a stroke of white paint down the edge of long balloons. Use different words to describe size as you go along.

MAKE A DISPLAY
Turn the work into a display with headings and labels, as with the colour and shape balloons.

ASSESSMENT
Colour: look out for the child's ability to recognise, match and name the colours. How much help does she need with tying and untying the balloons?
Shape: look out for the child's ability to recognise the different shapes and, later, name them. Can older children draw and cut out their own shapes?
Size: look out for the child's ability to discriminate between the different sizes and dimensions and, later, to name them.

EARLY LEARNING GOALS
Knowledge and Understanding of the World:
Investigate objects and materials by using all of their senses as appropriate.
Find out about, and identify, some features of living things, objects and events they observe.
Look closely at similarities, differences, pattern and change.

Mathematical Development:
Use language such as 'circle' or 'bigger' to describe the shape and size of solids and flat shapes.
Communication, Language and Literacy:
Interact with others, negotiating plans and activities and taking turns in conversation.
Extend their vocabulary.
Physical Development:
Handle tools, objects, construction and malleable materials safely and with increasing control.

A C T I V I T Y - *Sorting balloons*

ABOUT THE ACTIVITY
This is a sorting activity based on the balloon theme and using colour, size and shape as sorting criteria. The balloon is a useful object for sorting as its shape, size and colour can easily be adapted. For sorting large/small and colour, you can use real balloons. Shape is more easily covered by cutting out paper balloons (see below).

Sorting involves being able to recognise differences and similarities and put objects into groups, according to whatever sorting criteria is being used. It is a useful activity for helping the child learn to recognise different qualities.

GROUP
Any number for introducing and showing the activity. Preferably no more than two at a time for working independently.

WHAT YOU WILL NEED
Real balloons in a variety of colours and different sizes *or* sets of cut-out balloons. Choose from some or all of the following:

◆ Large and small balloons in various colours - such as three small red, three large red, three small blue, three large blue and so on.

◆ Thin and fat balloons in various colours - such as three fat green and three thin green, three fat yellow and three thin yellow, and so on.

◆ Long and short balloons in various colours - such as three long purple and three short purple, three long orange and three short orange, and so on.

Different shapes, such as three pink square balloons, three brown circular balloons, three white triangular balloons. If you wish to add other sorting criteria to this set you could make them different colours and sizes.

Something for the children to sort into. Either cut out large paper balloons corresponding with the balloons to be sorted or glue matching balloons on to cardboard boxes.

WHAT TO DO
Choose the set or sets you want the children to sort. Limit or extend the choices depending on age and developmental level. For example, a simple sorting would consist of two or three balloons in two different colours. A complex sorting might be large, medium and small balloons in red, yellow, blue, green, orange and purple - using the sorting criteria of size to create three different groups.

Put out the appropriate mats or boxes. For your simple sorting, this would be two large balloon shapes cut out of red and yellow sugar paper or card. For your complex sorting, you would need a large balloon shape, a medium balloon shape and a small balloon shape, preferably in a neutral colour that does not correspond with the colours of your sorting balloons. This highlights that the sorting criteria is size rather than colour.

Show the children what to do, using the appropriate describing words as much as possible. Draw them into the activity and leave them to carry on independently, preferably in groups of no more than two.

MAKE A DISPLAY
If you have made a display in connection with sizes, shapes and colours, link the sorting groups with groups of balloons in the display.

ASSESSMENT
Look out for signs that the child can recognise similarities and differences of colour, shape and size and sort the objects accordingly. Can she organise her own work? Make a note of each child's ability to name the different colours.

EARLY LEARNING GOALS
Communication, Language and Literacy:
Interact with others, negotiating plans and activities and taking turns in conversation.
Knowledge and Understanding of the World:
Look closely at similarities, differences and change.
Mathematical Development:
Use language such as 'circle' or 'bigger' to describe the shape and size of solids and flat shapes.
Creative Development:
Explore colour, texture, shape, form and space in two or three dimensions.

ACTIVITY - *Where will the balloon take you?*

ABOUT THE ACTIVITY
The magical blue balloon takes the little boy and Kipper on a trip into space. They land on a planet, make friends with some aliens and then get back home in time for tea.
This activity challenges the children to think about where they might go with the magical blue balloon. It gives them a framework in which to use their imagination and create a different story. It requires them to use language in order to describe their story and, through you writing down their thoughts, it gives them the opportunity to see the purpose and process of writing.

One of the advantages of this kind of activity is that children can respond at their own level. Be prepared for children who simply retell the adventure in the book. Although they may not have created their own story, they will still have had a valuable oral language experience, requiring them to remember, put their thoughts in order and use oral language to express themselves in front of the group.

GROUP
Four or five children.

WHAT YOU WILL NEED
A clip-board and marker pen
The Blue Balloon
Paper and pencils or paint for pictures
White paper for writing
Paper to make a group book

WHAT TO DO
Look at the part of the story that shows the boy floating off into space, on openings 11, 12 and 13.
Introduce the idea of imagining where the children would like to go: 'Charlie, where would you like the blue balloon to take you?' Start off by asking a verbal child or give some ideas of your own. Ask the child questions as you go along to help her develop her story. Encourage her to end by getting back home in time for tea or some other purpose. This helps the child to finish off her little story and highlights the concept of 'the ending'.

With your clip-board and marker pen, make a note of the children's ideas, writing down their own words as much as possible. Explain to them what you are doing and let them see you writing, to help them develop a sense of the process and purpose of writing.

MAKE A DISPLAY

Ask the children to make pictures of their magical journeys. Write up their different journeys, asking any children who are ready to help with the writing. Compile the pictures and writing into a group book.

ASSESSMENT

Look out for how fluently the child can put her thoughts into words. Is she re-telling the story or creating her own story? What range of vocabulary does she use, and how complex is her sentence structure? How confidently can she speak in front of the group and is she showing signs of being aware of her listeners? Is she able to finish off her story or does she need prompting from the adult?

EARLY LEARNING GOALS

Communication, Language and Literacy:
Enjoy listening to and using spoken and written language, and readily turn to it in their play and learning.
Speak clearly and audibly with confidence and control and show awareness of the listener.
Listen with enjoyment, respond to stories and make up their own stories.
Use language to imagine and recreate roles and experiences.
Retell narratives in the correct sequence, drawing on language patterns of stories.
Show an understanding of the elements of stories, such as main character, sequence of events, and openings.
Creative Development:
Use their imagination in role play and stories.
Personal, Social and Emotional Development:
Maintain attention, concentrate and sit quietly when appropriate.

FIVE-MINUTE ACTIVITIES

FIVE FAT BALLOONS

Sing the following song with the children, to the tune of 'Five fat sausages frying in a pan'. If you prefer, the words can be recited rather than sung:

Five fat balloons tied to a string
Puff puff puff
One went zing
Four fat balloons tied to a string
Puff puff puff
Another went bang

Three fat balloons tied to a string
Puff puff puff
A third went ping

Two fat balloons tied to a string
Puff puff puff
The next went bang

One fat balloon tied to a string
That went pop
And then there were none

Have five children holding a balloon each. When their balloon goes zing, bang, ping or pop, they can pass it to a helper and go and sit down. Give other children in the group percussion instruments to make the sounds.

STRETCH, SQUEEZE AND SQUASH

Show the children opening 7 where the little boy and Kipper try to burst the balloon. Give the children a cushion each and practise the various actions - stretching, squeezing, squashing. Explain that you are pretending the cushion is a balloon (you could use real balloons but it is rather disturbing if they do burst!)

Turn the activity into a listen and action game by playing music for the children to dance to. When the music stops, they must listen to your instruction - 'squeeze your balloon' - and perform the action. Depending on your group, you may prefer to leave out actions such as wacking and kicking and introduce some alternatives such as 'patting', 'stroking', 'cuddling', 'shaking'. Emphasise to the children that they must listen carefully for when the music starts again - this is the signal to end their action and dance again.

FIND THE BALLOON

Follow a similar format to 'Find Grandpa's handkerchief' (see page 28). Chalk balloon shapes on the playground - different sizes or shapes or colours. Link with the 'Sorting balloons' activity by holding up a cut-out balloon for the children to find and stand in.

About Washing Line

Washing Line is a bright, cheerful flap book suitable for children from about two-and-a-half onwards.

The washing line of the title has five oddly-shaped garments hanging from it. Elephant is the central character with the task of finding the owners of the garments. Each owner turns out to be an animal, hiding behind the sturdy flaps and wearing the garment so that the children can see how the two go together. The long thin socks belong to the flamingo, the jumper with long arms belongs to the orang-utan, the tiny dress belongs to the mouse, the giraffe owns the long scarf, and the elephant himself owns the big, spotty shorts.

The repetitive text is based on the ever popular question/answer format, making it easy for the children to join in: *Whose are those socks hanging on the washing line? Asked the elephant. They're mine said the flamingo.*

The simple but cleverly structured story incorporates the three themes of matching, size and number sequence (1 to 5).

A C T I V I T Y - *Exploring clothes*

ABOUT THE ACTIVITY
This activity builds on the clothing theme in the *Washing Line* story by linking clothes with the weather. Exploring clothes in this way introduces an element of sorting because you will be grouping clothes according to their similarities and differences.

Bear in mind that young children won't necessarily remember the different seasons and weathers. Keep your approach simple, sticking to hot weather, cold weather and rainy weather. As always, link your exploration to their real experiences as much as possible.

GROUP
Four or five children.

WHAT YOU WILL NEED
Different clothes linking with different weathers:

◆ Cold weather clothes - woolly hats, scarves, gloves, boots.
◆ Rainy weather clothes - cagoule, sou'wester, wellies, umbrella.
◆ Hot weather clothes - shorts, sun hat, sunglasses, T-shirt, swimsuit.

Pictures of winter scenes, rainy scenes and hot weather scenes.

WHAT TO DO
Encourage the children to feel the clothes, name them and talk about when we wear these kinds of clothes and why. Can they remember the relevant weathers? Was there a rainy day recently? How did it feel when they went to the seaside in the summer holidays/built a snowman in the garden when it snowed? What did they wear? Invite them to try on the clothes. How do they feel? Think about why we have different types of material. Why do we wear woolly clothes in winter and thin cotton in summer? Test one of the rainy weather garments and a T-shirt with water to discover why

the former is suitable for rainy weather. Give the children a pile of rainy/hot or hot/cold or rainy/cold clothes or all three types to sort into separate boxes according to the weather group they fall into.

MAKE A DISPLAY
With the children, make a background to reflect the appropriate weather. For example, sponge print white splodges onto pale grey paper, stick on cotton-wool balls and/or cut out snowflakes from circles of white paper. Pin the winter clothes to the background. Ask the children to help you plan a heading, explaining that we wear these clothes in winter. Add the heading and written labels for each garment.

Take a similar approach with rainy and hot weather clothes. Make rainy or hot backgrounds to pin the clothes onto.

ASSESSMENT
Look out for how much the child remembers about each season and its weather. Can the child recognise the qualities and features of the hot weather/cold weather/rainy weather clothes and sort them accordingly? Is the older child able to recognise why different garments are appropriate for different types of weather?

EARLY LEARNING GOALS
Knowledge and Understanding of the World:
Investigate objects and materials by using all of their senses as appropriate.
Look closely at similarities, differences, patterns and change.
Find out about their environment, and talk about those features they like and dislike.
Communication, Language and Literacy:
Interact with others, negotiating plans and activities and taking turns in conversation.

A C T I V I T Y - *Matching animals and garments*

ABOUT THE ACTIVITY

In the book, the matching of animals and garments happens within the story and pictures. The child witnesses the matching but does not participate. This activity gives children the chance to choose for themselves which animal should go with which garment, and put the two together. To do this, the child needs to think about sizes and shapes and make a logical connection between the animal and its garment, for example the *tall* neck of the giraffe matching the *long* scarf. This makes the activity more complex than matching two things that are identical, such as two blue circles.

GROUP

Up to four children at a time for the art/craft part of the activity. No more than five for the matching activity.

WHAT YOU WILL NEED

Washing Line
Sugar paper, paint, paint brushes, printing materials and sponge printing pad, collage materials, glue
String to make a washing line, clothes pegs, washing basket (optional)

WHAT TO DO

◆ **MAKING THE ANIMALS AND GARMENTS:** look at the animals and garments in *Washing Line*. Give the children one or two animal and/or garment shapes cut out from sugar paper. Any children who are ready can be encouraged to draw and cut out the shapes for themselves. Alternatively, give them templates to draw around and cut out. If possible, choose appropriate colours - yellow for the giraffe, grey for the elephant, white for the mouse.

Choose some appropriate printing, painting or collage techniques to decorate the animal or garment:
◆ half a potato to print the giraffe's spots
◆ a string block with lengths of string glued closely together to print the orang-utan's hair and the woollen garments
◆ sponge printing for the elephant's rough, wrinkly skin
◆ gluing on strips, circles or scraps of fabric to make the various garments

Try out the different techniques with the children and encourage them to choose what they think is most suitable for a particular animal. Let them explore and enjoy the materials - this is much more important than having a perfectly spotted giraffe. Once the animal has been completed, show the children how to add eyes, mouth and nostrils. Leave the animals and garments to dry and then decorate on the other side.

◆ **MATCHING THE ANIMALS AND GARMENTS:** pick one of each animal and one of each garment from the *Washing Line* story. Choose the most robust and ask the child's permission to use their work or make your own using the same techniques. If the children do not need too much support from you, they will enjoy seeing you work alongside them.

It is fun to rig up a washing line - between the legs of an upturned table or on the climbing frame if you can play this outside. Put the clothes pegs in a basket and place the garments in a washing basket. Ask a child to choose an animal. Ask her to find the matching garment in the washing basket and peg it to the line. Give help with using the pegs if necessary, particularly when it comes to protecting the garment. Proceed until all the animals/garments have been matched.

MAKE A DISPLAY

Display the work on large sheets of pale blue and green paper to represent the sky and the grass. Pin up a length of string and hang the garments from the washing line. Blu-tack the animals beneath the washing line and add a notice - 'Can you match the animals with their clothes?'

EXTENSION

This activity can be extended by making and then matching extra animals and garments. In this way, you will be stretching the children's ability to match because they will not be able to rely on their memories of the story. It also enables you to introduce new matching criteria such as colour and texture.
◆ a zebra and a stripy hat
◆ a sheep and a white woolly cardigan
◆ a leopard and four spotty wellies
◆ a camel and a coat with a big hump on the back

ASSESSMENT

Art activity: look out for how well the children handle scissors, glue and printing techniques (see Assessment for 'Animal flaps' page 30 and 'Printing handkerchiefs' page 28) Are older children able to choose appropriate techniques to decorate animals and garments?

Matching activity: does the younger child understand how to carry out the activity? How well can she discriminate between size and shape and match the animal with its garment? Can she meet the physical challenges of pegging the clothes to the washing line?

EARLY LEARNING GOALS

Creative Development:
Explore colour, texture, shape, form and space in two or three dimensions.
Knowledge and Understanding of the World:
Look closely at similarities, differences, patterns and change.
Mathematical Development:
Use language such as 'bigger' to describe the shape and size of solids and flat shapes.
Use everyday words to describe position.
Physical Development:
Handle tools, objects, construction and malleable materials safely and with increasing control.
Use a range of small and large equipment.
Communication, Language and Literacy:
Interact with others, negotiating plans and activities and taking turns in conversation.

ACTIVITY - *Washing line number sequence*

ABOUT THIS ACTIVITY

The number sequence in *Washing Line* consists of the animal groups increasing one by one. The structure of the book is used to show how the number sequence builds up. At the start of the story, the left-hand page shows one animal (opening 3). Turn the flap and there is a second animal on the right-hand page. Turn the page and there are two animals on the left-hand page. Turn the flap again and we are introduced to a third animal. Turn the page and there are the three animals - and so on.

The text also creates a sequence in words by listing the animal names, adding one more each time. On the first page of the story (opening 3) the words are: 'Whose are those socks hanging on the washing line? asked the **elephant**.' On the next full page (opening 5): 'Whose is that jumper hanging on the washing line? asked the **elephant** and the **flamingo**.' (Bold type added.)

This activity explores the theme of number groups from one to five through counting the groups and making a number sequence display. Setting out the groups of animals in a triangular format shows the children the number of units that makes up each separate quantity - from a group of one to a group of five. It also shows that each group has one more animal than the group before. Writing the number symbol beside each group shows the sequence of symbols - 1, 2, 3, 4, 5 - as well as showing each symbol along with the quantity it represents.

GROUP

No more than five children.

WHAT YOU WILL NEED

Washing Line
Animals made by the children, using the techniques described in the 'Matching animals and garments' activity. You will need five elephants, four flamingos, three orang-utans, two mice and one giraffe.
A sheet of paper large enough to accommodate the animals (the back of a wallpaper roll is a good size to use, but avoid ready-pasted).
Blu-tack and marker pen.

WHAT TO DO

Look at the *Washing Line* story. Point to and count the animals on each page - 'one' (elephant) on opening 3; 'one, two' (elephant and flamingo) on opening 5; 'one, two, three' (elephant, flamingo and orang-utan) on opening 7, and so on. Start from 'one' each time. Encourage the children to join in as much as possible with pointing and counting.

Spread out the paper and ask a child to give you one elephant. Put a piece of Blu-tack on the back and show the child where to attach the elephant - at the top of the paper on the left-hand side to the top of the paper. Point to the elephant, count 'one' and use the

marker pen to write the symbol 1 beside the elephant. If you have a child who is ready, ask him or her to write the numbers.

Ask another child to bring you an elephant and a flamingo. Show the child where to stick them on the paper so that the elephants are directly above each other. Count them, 'one, two'. Write the symbol 2 beside the flamingo.

Continue until the fifth group made up of five animals has been stuck onto the paper and the symbol 5 written beside them. The animals should form the shape of a right-angled triangle. Make sure they are arranged so that each animal has a clear space, to make it obvious to the children that each line is longer by *one* animal (see diagram).

MAKE A DISPLAY

Put up the number sequence on the wall and encourage the children to count the groups of animals and count the symbols 1 to 5.

ASSESSMENT

Look out for the child's ability to count each quantity. Can she count in sequence and match each quantity with its symbol?

EARLY LEARNING GOALS

Mathematical Development:
Say and use number names in order in familiar contexts.
Count reliably up to 10 everyday objects.
Recognise numerals 1 to 9.
In practical activities and discussion begin to use the vocabulary involved in adding and subtracting.
Find one more or one less than a number from one to 10.

Communication, Language and Literacy:
Interact with others, negotiating plans and activities and taking turns in conversation.

ACTIVITY - *Size and opposites*

ABOUT THE ACTIVITY

Size is a complex topic. Like colour, size is a concept rather than an object. Unlike colour, size is always relative. It has no absolute meaning in the sense that red is always red whereas an object is only big if compared with something smaller. In other words, a house is big when compared to a garden shed but small when compared to a cathedral.

This means that size is best looked at with young children in terms of opposites or contrasts. If you make a display of small objects, you also need to have a display of big objects; if you make a display of long objects, you also need a display of short objects.

The *Washing Line* story presents the size concepts big / small and long or tall / short. As these are two of the most obvious size concepts for the young child to recognise, the book makes a useful starting point for an exploration of size.

GROUP

Four or five children.

WHAT YOU WILL NEED

Washing Line
A selection of everyday big/small objects and long or tall/short objects
Two trays or mats
Display labels with the words 'big', 'small', 'long', 'short'
A large table for displaying the objects

WHAT TO DO

Big/small: Look at the following in the *Washing Line* story:

◆ The big elephant on opening 3 and the small mouse on opening 9.
◆ The big shorts on opening 11 and the tiny dress on opening 7.
◆ The shorts and the dress side by side on the washing line on opening 16.
◆ The big ears of the elephant and the little ears of the orang-utan on opening 16.

Use the words 'big' and 'little' as much as possible. If you have made mice, elephants, dresses and pants as part of the previous activities, compare these also.

Gather a selection of everyday objects, preferably pairs of similar objects in different sizes. For example:

◆ A bumper-sized crisp packet/a small crisp packet
◆ A giant Smartie/a tiny Smartie
◆ A big leaf/a small leaf
◆ An individual juice carton/a family-sized juice carton

Look at the objects with the children. Talk about them freely. Depending on the age and language development of your group, introduce other size words as part of your general conversation (tiny, little, large, huge, giant sized). Put out two mats or trays on the floor and show the children how to sort the objects into the two categories, small and big. Place the cards saying 'small' and 'big' beside the two categories. Although we are not expecting children to read the words at this stage, any opportunity to look at and absorb written language is valuable.

MAKE A DISPLAY

Display the two groups of objects on a table. Make the display interactive by putting two or three new pairs of objects into a box for the children to sort into their correct groups. Maintain interest by adding new objects every couple of days.

EXTEND THE DISPLAY

Encourage the children to find pairs of objects to add to the display - a useful little challenge to set children when playing in the garden, sorting through the building block box or exploring the book corner. Send a note home explaining the activity and asking parents to help their children find pairs of objects, one big, one small. If necessary, give suggestions for objects that are easy to find in two sizes - coins, stamps, books, pencils, cups, plates, toothbrushes, dolls, toy cars. Encourage those children who are ready to draw a small and a big house/car/cat and so on. Younger ones can simply draw on a small piece of paper and a big piece of paper to add to the display.

Long/short: Look at the following in the *Washing Line* story:

◆ The long legs of the flamingo on opening 4 and the short legs of the mouse on opening 9.
◆ The long arms of the orang-utan on opening 6 and the short arms of the mouse on opening 9.
◆ The long neck of the giraffe on opening 10 and the short neck of the orang-utan on opening 6.
◆ The long socks, the long arms on the jumper, the long scarf and the short dress on the washing line on opening 16.

Talk about them and use the words 'long' or 'tall' and 'short' to describe them.

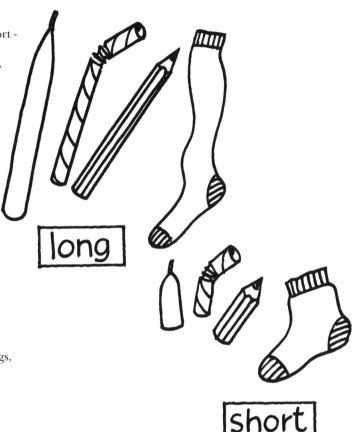

Choose everyday objects to represent long or tall and short - candles, pencils, a toilet roll and a kitchen towel roll, spaghetti, ribbons, paint brushes, combs, drinking straws, the arms of a child's jumper and an adult's jumper.

Continue with exploration, sorting and display in the same way as big/small.

ASSESSMENT

How well can the child discriminate between big/small and tall/short? Is she able to recognise these qualities in the environment by finding items to add to the collection? Look out for occasions when the child uses the appropriate language to describe the qualities.

EARLY LEARNING GOALS

Communication, Language and Literacy:
Interact with others, negotiating plans and activities and taking turns in conversation.
Knowledge and Understanding of the World:
Look closely at similarities, differences and change.
Find out about, and identify, some features of living things, objects and events they observe.
Mathematical Development:
Use language such as 'circle' or 'bigger' to describe the shape and size of solids and flat shapes.

FIVE-MINUTE ACTIVITIES

SIMILES

The instructions in the 'Animal small, animal tall' game are similes - they fit into the language format of 'as ..... as a ......' or '..... like a .....'

Once the children have grasped the size concepts of big/small and long or tall/short, challenge them to come up with similes. Start them off with a few of your own: as tall as a tree; as tall as a house; as tall as the door. This language game can either be played sitting in a group or slipped into some free moments chatting to the children in the garden or at snack time.

ANIMAL SMALL, ANIMAL TALL

Play music with an animal theme for the children to dance to. When you stop the music the children have to stand still and listen for their

instruction. Choose from 'Make yourself as tall as a giraffe / big as a hippo / small as a mouse / long trunk like an elephant / thin as a snake / fat as a piglet.'

Go through the different instructions you are planning to use and discuss with the children how they are going to make themselves thin/tall and so on. If necessary, have a helper join in with the actions to support the younger ones.

WASHING LINE FEELY BAG

This game can be played with any reasonably sized group but the children must be able to name different garments.

Have a big laundry bag. Place a garment into the bag and ask a child

to feel it and decide what it is. Make sure the garments are small and distinctive - a glove, a woolly hat, a sock, a small cardigan.

Alternatively, give the child a garment to feel and then find the matching garment in the bag.

About The Very Hungry Caterpillar

The Very Hungry Caterpillar is a picture book classic. It was first published in 1970 and has become one of the best loved children's books of all time.

Like all good picture books, it is very simple yet, at the same time, offers a rich variety of early learning opportunities. Most important of all, it is a riot of colour and fun with subtle touches of humour here and there (look at the expression on the caterpillar's face after he has munched his way through a piece of chocolate cake, one ice cream cone, one pickle, one salami, one slice of Swiss cheese...)

The three main themes in the story are number, one to five; days of the week (incorporating sequence) and the life-cycle of the butterfly (including the concepts of change and difference.)

A C T I V I T Y - *Painted collage*

ABOUT THE ACTIVITY

Eric Carle uses a distinctive but simple art technique to create his eye-catching illustrations. If you look carefully at his pictures, you can see the paint-brush strokes and different paint effects. He then cuts or tears his decorated papers into smaller pieces to make collage. Most of Eric Carle's techniques can also be used by the children to create pictures of a similar style.

GROUP

Up to four children.

WHAT YOU WILL NEED

Thick paint; brushes
Different coloured sugar paper
Strips of thick card, cut into a comb shape
Scissors
Glue
Tissue paper

WHAT TO DO

Explain to the children that the pictures in *The Very Hungry Caterpillar* were painted by somebody called Eric Carle. Look at the pictures and show the children the brush strokes, the patterns in the paint and the sharp or rough edges where he has cut or torn out the collage pieces.

Provide the children with thick brushes, thick paint and sugar paper. Choose just two or three colours of paper and paint in contrasting combinations - red paint on green paper, red paint on yellow paper. Look again at the book and then show the children some or all of the following techniques:

♦ Make thick brush strokes randomly across the paper to create the same effect as the big yellow sun on opening 5. Encourage the children to keep on painting until the brush is just about dry as this will ensure that the brush strokes show through.

♦ Show the children how to load their brush with paint and press down sideways on the paper to create a fan shape. Repeat until the paint is used up.

♦ Show the children how to stab down with the brush to get a stippled effect - you may wish to use old, worn brushes as this is not very good for the bristles. Use two different colours, waiting for the first to dry before using the second to get an effect like the oranges on opening 10.

♦ Mix paint with flour. Paint thickly onto the paper and then comb with a plastic comb or strip of card cut into teeth to create a similar effect to the sky background on opening 4.

Once dry, show the children how to cut their paintings into pieces. They will find it easier to cut from smaller pieces of paper so begin by cutting the original paintings into halves or quarters. They can then either cut randomly or draw around shapes to cut out. If they have difficulty drawing and cutting randomly, draw shapes for them. You can also show them how to tear the paper to get an interesting edge, but bear in mind that young children cannot tear with control.

Once they have lots of pieces, provide them with large sheets of paper. Brilliant white is the most effective for setting off the bright colours of the paint. Show the children how to choose different shapes and colours to stick onto their white background. Encourage the older ones to arrange and rearrange the pieces before sticking. The easiest gluing technique for this kind of activity is to put a blob of glue onto the background (not too much) and then place the collage piece on top.

If you have older children with good hand control, you could try working on tissue paper. Use the same technique but add a small quantity of water if your paint is thick.

MAKE A DISPLAY

Display the children's work with a written label explaining that you have made pictures like Eric Carle's illustrations in *The Very Hungry Caterpillar.*

These techniques can also be used for making the life-cycle of a butterfly display (see page 52) and a number sequence like that in the story (see page 54).

ASSESSMENT
Look out for how closely the child observes the pictures in *The Very Hungry Caterpillar*. How successfully is she able to use the techniques that you show her? Look out also for how the children handle scissors and glue (see Assessment for 'Animal flaps' page 30).

EARLY LEARNING GOALS
Creative Development:

Explore colour, texture, shape, form and space in two or three dimensions.
Use their imagination in art and design.
Express and communicate their ideas, thoughts and feelings by using a widening range of materials, suitable tools ... designing and making.
Knowledge and Understanding of the World:
Look closely at similarities, differences, patterns and change
Mathematical Development:
Talk about, recognise and recreate simple patterns.
Physical Development:
Handle tools, objects, construction and malleable materials safely and with increasing control.

ACTIVITY- *Making butterflies*

ABOUT THE ACTIVITY
Butterflies make a good subject for art work. You can use a specific technique for decorating the wings or leave the children free to paint them in whatever way they wish. The butterfly on opening 14 makes a particularly colourful starting point for this activity.

GROUP
Up to four children.

WHAT YOU WILL NEED
Sugar paper; typing paper; tissue paper
Thick paint and paint brushes in different colours
Wax shavings and lumps of wax
A warm iron
Toilet roll tubes
Pipe-cleaners

WHAT TO DO
Look at the butterfly at the end of *The Very Hungry Caterpillar*. Look at pictures of real butterflies. Talk about the shape of their wings and their different colours. Choose a book on butterflies to give you and the children further information. Adapt the information you give to suit the age and developmental level of your children. Use a basic butterfly template to draw round and cut out and then choose one or more of the following techniques for decorations:

◆ Put thick blobs of paint onto one wing. Fold the wings over and place a large piece of paper or tea towel on top. Show the child how to press down firmly to spread the paint. Open up and enjoy the patterns.
◆ Make your butterfly shapes from white typing paper. Give the children chunks and shavings of wax crayon to sprinkle onto one wing. Fold over the other wing, place a tea towel on top and press with a warm iron. The warm iron melts the shavings so that they run together, creating beautiful patterns. If you can do this while the children watch, they will enjoy seeing the change that takes place in the wax but make sure that another adult is

supervising them while you iron. When the wax is dry, paint over the back of the paper with cooking oil. This makes the butterfly translucent so that it glows like stained glass when displayed on the window.

◆ Make your butterfly shapes from white paper and glue torn or cut pieces of tissue paper in different colours. Overlap the shapes to create new colours and shades, like the butterfly on opening 14 of *The Very Hungry Caterpillar*.

To make the butterfly's body, show the children how to paint an empty toilet paper roll. For a thinner, smaller body, staple a rectangle of coloured paper to make a cylinder. Glue on eyes and attach pipe-cleaners for the antennae.

MAKE A DISPLAY
Attach your butterflies randomly to the wall as if they are fluttering about. Cut out some large green leaves as a background. Display wax butterflies against a sunny window.

ASSESSMENT
Look out for how creatively the child can use the different techniques to make her butterfly. How well can she handle scissors and glue? (see Assessment for 'Animal flaps' page 30).

EARLY LEARNING GOALS
Creative Development:
Explore colour, texture, shape, form and space in two or three dimensions.
Use their imagination in art and design.
Express and communicate their ideas, thoughts and feelings by using a widening range of materials, suitable tools ... designing and making.
Knowledge and Understanding of the World:
Look closely at similarities, differences, patterns and change.
Mathematical Development:
Talk about, recognise and recreate simple patterns.
Physical Development:
Handle tools, objects, construction and malleable materials safely and with increasing control.

ACTIVITY - *The life-cycle of a butterfly*

ABOUT THE ACTIVITY

The Very Hungry Caterpillar makes the perfect starting point for looking at the life-cycle of a butterfly. As the story progresses from its beginning to its end, it works through the stages of the life-cycle in clear order. Although the story has fantasy elements, it includes a number of accurate and accessible facts:

◆ Butterflies lay their eggs on leaves.
◆ Caterpillars eat constantly.
◆ The cocoon acts as a house where the caterpillar stays for about two weeks.
◆ The caterpillar emerges from the cocoon transformed into a beautiful butterfly.

GROUP

Up to six children, depending on level of support needed.

WHAT YOU WILL NEED

The Very Hungry Caterpillar
Copies of the photocopiable illustrations showing the stages in the life-cycle (page 88)
Large paper circle
Scissors, glue, coloured pencils or crayons
Painted collage pieces and butterfly from 'Making butterflies' activity (optional)
Clip-board, plain paper, marker pen
Bug viewer

The life cycle of a butterfly

WHAT TO DO

Use *The Very Hungry Caterpillar* story to look at and talk about the different stages in the butterfly's life-cycle. Pick out the facts in the story to highlight to the children. Compare the tiny white egg at the beginning of the story (opening 4) with the huge brightly-coloured butterfly at the end (opening 14). Introduce describing words to highlight the changes that take place in the caterpillar - the *tiny* egg, the *huge* butterfly; the *small* caterpillar, the *big, fat* caterpillar; the *white* egg, the *brightly* coloured butterfly.

If possible, find a caterpillar to look at. Scoop up the caterpillar with a leaf. Place it in a clear plastic bug viewer with a magnifier in the top so that the children can look without having to handle it. Talk about the caterpillar's colour and the importance of camouflage. Observe the way in which it moves. Return it to its habitat as soon as possible.

Give the children a photocopy of the four stages in a butterfly's cycle - egg, caterpillar, chrysalis and butterfly (see page 88). Name and talk about each stage then ask the children to cut them out, put them in their correct order and stick them onto a strip of paper. Better still, ask the children to make their own drawings of the four stages, using the photocopy or the book as a guide if they need to.

MAKE A DISPLAY

Display the different stages on a chart reflecting the circular nature of the butterfly's life-cycle (see illustration). Encourage the children to explain what is happening from one stage to the next.

Make labels to describe each stage. Get out your clip-board, paper and marker pen and ask the children to help you decide what to write. Encourage their responses by asking certain key questions, drawing on the information they will have gathered from *The Very Hungry Caterpillar* and your discussion. Use the book to check back if necessary and come up with labels such as 'The hungry caterpillar eats lots of green leaves' and 'The butterfly nibbles out of the chrysalis'. Stick these onto the circle. Involve the children with the cutting and sticking as much as possible. If you have any writers, ask them to help with writing labels.

ASSESSMENT

Look out for the signs that the child is absorbing the information you give about the butterfly's life-cycle. Does she contribute to the discussion with questions and comments? How closely does she observe the caterpillar?

When you make the life-cycle chart, ask the child to explain what is happening in each stage. This is a good way of assessing her understanding of the process.

EARLY LEARNING GOALS

Knowledge and Understanding of the World:
Investigate objects and materials by using all of their senses as appropriate.
Observe, find out about and identify features in the place they live and the natural world.
Look closely at similarities, differences, patterns and change.
Ask questions about why things happen and how things work.
Communication, Language and Literacy:
Enjoy listening to and using spoken and written language, and readily turn to it in their play and learning.
Sustain attentive listening, responding to what they have heard by relevant comments, questions or actions.
Extend their vocabulary.
Physical Development:
Handle tools, objects, construction and malleable materials safely and with increasing control.

A C T I V I T Y- *Menus for a very hungry caterpillar*

ABOUT THE ACTIVITY

There are two aspects to the Very Hungry Caterpillar. On the one hand he goes through all the normal stages in the butterfly's life-cycle, giving the children some useful lessons in natural history. On the other hand, Eric Carle has given free rein to his imagination to create a fantasy creature - no real caterpillar would munch his way through cup cakes, lollipops and salami! While the story makes a useful starting point for studying butterflies, it is also fun to concentrate on the fantasy element. This activity encourages the children to think about different foods and make up some new menus for the Very Hungry Caterpillar.

The sequence of weekdays is yet another concept presented by the book. Each day is given its own page. As the week progresses day by day, the number of fruits eaten by the caterpillar increases and the pages get longer. This reflects the days of the week as a series, building up one by one until you have the whole week made up of seven days.

GROUP

Up to seven children for planning the week's menu, three or four at a time for making the display.

WHAT YOU WILL NEED

The Very Hungry Caterpillar
A clip-board, paper and marker pen
Pictures of foods or drawing/painting materials for the children to make their own
Scissors
Glue
Seven pieces of background paper
Paper for writing labels.

WHAT TO DO

Look at the pictures of the foods that the Very Hungry Caterpillar ate on Saturday. Name them and find out which ones the children have tried. Bring in samples of the foods that may not be familiar to them - the pickle (try gherkins), Swiss cheese (try Emmenthal), salami and water melon. Allow the children to taste them, checking first for allergies, vegetarianism and cultural food restrictions. Some children are unwilling to try new foods - encourage them to sniff and touch instead.

Create your own week's menu for the Very Hungry Caterpillar, linking it with the days of the week. Have ready your clip-board, paper and marker pen and explain to the children that you are going to think of some new foods for the caterpillar to try. 'What did the Very Hungry Caterpillar eat on Monday?' Ask a child to suggest a food and write it down.'What did the Very Hungry Caterpillar eat on Tuesday?' Ask a child to suggest a food and write it down. Read through the results: 'On Monday the Very Hungry Caterpillar ate fish fingers. On Tuesday the Very Hungry Caterpillar ate baked beans ....' If you have lots of children

in your group, the caterpillar can eat more than one food item on each day.

MAKE A DISPLAY

Make a display with the children, showing the Very Hungry Caterpillar's new menu and the days of the week. Bring in pictures of the foods for the children to cut out and stick onto a sheet of background paper, one for each day of the week. Use the labels from tins and packets or magazine pictures. Alternatively, ask the children to draw and paint their own pictures to cut out. Talk about the different foods with the children as you go along. Make a written explanation for each sheet - 'On Monday, the Very Hungry Caterpillar ate ....'. Ask any writers to help out with explanations, headings and labels.

ASSESSMENT

How do the children react to tasting the different foods? Encourage them to respond in words and facial expression so that you can assess what they are gaining from the activity. How readily can they think of items for the caterpillar's new menu? Observe how the child handles scissors and glue (see Assessment for 'Animal flaps' page 30). Once you have set up the display, make a note of how well the children are able to go through the days of the week.

EARLY LEARNING GOALS

Knowledge and Understanding of the World:
Investigate objects and materials by using all of their senses as appropriate.
Observe, find out about and identify features in the place they live and the natural world.
Communication, Language and Literacy:
Enjoy listening to and using spoken and written language, and readily turn to it in their play and learning.
Sustain attentive listening, responding to what they have heard by relevant comments, questions or actions.
Extend their vocabulary.
Physical Development:
Recognise the importance of keeping healthy and those things which contribute to this.
Handle tools, objects, construction and malleable materials safely and with increasing control.

ACTIVITY - *Making a number sequence*

ABOUT THE ACTIVITY

Number is the third main theme of *The Very Hungry Caterpillar*. The middle pages have been cleverly cut in order to present the number groups from one to five. Each page gets longer to accommodate the increase in number. This means that the child can see the groups of objects increase by one (one apple, two pears, three plums, four strawberries, five oranges) and see that each group gets larger because the pages themselves get longer each time.

The organisation of the pages gives you the choice of counting the fruits from one to five; *one* (apple), *two* (apple and pear), *three* (apple, pear and plum); or it gives you the

option of looking at how each quantity is made up - one apple on the first page; two pears on the second page; three plums on the third page, and so on. Along with the pictures that *show* you what each quantity consists of, the text names each quantity.

GROUP

No more than five children.

WHAT TO DO

Make a number sequence based on the story, following a similar format to making a number sequence with the animals from *Washing Line* (see page 47). Use decorated papers from the 'Painted collage' activity and ask the children to cut out fruits. Display them on strips of paper increasing in length. For example, the Monday strip could be 20 cm long; the Tuesday strip 40 cm long, the Wednesday strip 60 cm long, right up to the Friday strip at 100 cm. 'Making a number sequence' can also be combined with the 'Menus' activity - use the children's own food suggestions rather than fruits - 'On Monday, the Very Hungry Caterpillar ate one baked bean; on Tuesday The Very Hungry Caterpillar ate two fish fingers...'

ASSESSMENT

Look out for the child's ability to count each quantity. Can she count in sequence and match each quantity with its symbol?

EARLY LEARNING GOALS

Mathematical Development:
Say and use number names in order in familiar contexts.
Count reliably up to 10 everyday objects.
Recognise numerals 1 to 9.
In practical activities and discussion begin to use the vocabulary involved in adding and subtracting.
Find one more or one less than a number from one to 10.
Communication, Language and Literacy:
Interact with others, negotiating plans and activities and taking turns in conversation.

FIVE-MINUTE ACTIVITIES

BE A BUTTERFLY

Show the children how to act out the four main stages in the butterfly's life-cycle: curling up in a tiny ball (egg); wriggling on the floor and 'nibbling' (caterpillar); crouching down and staying very still (chrysalis); fluttering their 'wings' (butterfly). Use *The Very Hungry Caterpillar* as a guide.

Play music for the children to dance to. When the music stops, name one of the stages for the children to perform. Start the music again as a sign for the children to finish their action and begin dancing again. If necessary, ask a helper to join in to remind the children of the actions.

TASTE TESTING

Have a selection of foods for children to taste when wearing a blindfold, to see if they can name the food from taste alone. Choose everyday, easily recognisable foods such as chunks of apple or bread. Some young children are reluctant to wear a blindfold or taste foods they are unsure of - do not force participation from an unwilling child.

WEEKLY DIARY

The Very Hungry Caterpillar can be used as the starting point for making a weekly diary with your group. See page 75 and follow the same process. Look at what the caterpillar eats on each day of the week as a lead into exploring your own weekly activities.

About Rosie's Walk

Rosie's Walk is another classic picture book. First published in 1968, it has intrigued and delighted children ever since.

The story is simple but clever. The words tell the straightforward tale of Rosie the hen's walk around the farmyard. The story consists of one long sentence lasting for the entire book: 'Rosie the hen went for a walk/across the yard/around the pond/over the haycock/past the mill/through the fence/under the beehives/and got back in time for dinner.' The pictures show a hungry fox, stalking Rosie and getting himself into all sorts of scrapes and accidents along the way.

The pictures are pure slapstick comedy. Every time the fox makes a leap at Rosie, he misses and lands in the pond .... in the haystack ..... on a stray rake which bashes him on the nose. The text makes no mention of the fox - the humour is purely visual.

The story can be taken on two levels. For very young children, it is just the tale of Rosie's walk around the farmyard. As the children's understanding of story develops, it becomes a much more complex story involving the interaction between Rosie and the fox. What is he up to? Will he get her in the end? Is Rosie really unaware of him or does she know him so well that she can be confident he will never succeed in catching up with her?
Keep your story group as small as possible and resist the temptation to point out the fox in the pictures. Make a note of when the children refer to him and what they say about him. This can tell you a lot about a child's developing ability to make sense of words and pictures.

Don't be put off by the illustrations. Although they seem a little dated by today's standards, Pat Hutchins has a unique style that can add variety to the child's experience of pictures. It is also useful for the child to see that a picture can have just three or four colours, as opposed to the visual feast of colour to be found in many more modern picture books.

ACTIVITY - Our walk

ABOUT THE ACTIVITY
The story of *Rosie's Walk* is dependent on prepositions or position words (across, around, over, past). Young children often find it difficult to grasp the meaning of these words. *Rosie's Walk* can be used as the starting point for activities to help the children understand:
◆ that everything has a position in relation to other things; and
◆ that there are words to describe these positions.

This activity involves the children creating their own walk around a familiar environment. The walk gives them active experience of various position words and also introduces simple orienteering skills. By following the format of *Rosie's Walk* in creating the story of their own walk, the activity enables them to participate in structuring a story:

◆ the beginning, when they set out on their walk;
◆ the progression of events as they walk through different parts of the room;
◆ the ending, when they return to where they started.

As you take your walk with the children, you can focus both on the position words used in the story: across, around, over, past, through and under. You can also introduce other words, such as beside, near, by, away from, close to.

GROUP
Keep as small as possible, ideally no more than three children.

WHAT YOU WILL NEED
Rosie's Walk
The classroom, garden or other environment that is familiar to the children
A clip-board, paper and marker pen
Paper, drawing things, scissors and glue

WHAT TO DO
Explain to your group that you are going to set off on a walk around the room, just like Rosie the hen taking her walk around the farmyard. Start out from a designated point that you will return to at the end of the walk, such as your group of chairs or the book corner. Encourage the children to decide the direction of the walk. You can give each child in the group a turn choosing where you go next. Introduce the appropriate position words as you go along - *around* the chairs, *across* the mats, *under* the pegs, *through* the cloakroom, *into* the toilets, *past* the chairs....

When you bring the walk to a close, try to make sure that you return to your starting point for a reason. Just as Rosie gets back to her hen coop in time for dinner, it helps to mark your ending if you can get back to the book corner in time for story, or the cloakroom in time for going out to play. Emphasise to the children that you have returned to the book corner/cloakroom in time for story/playtime.

Sit down with your group and go through where you went on your walk. Use clip-board and marker pen to make a note of the places and the appropriate position words.

Rosie's Walk

MAKE A DISPLAY

The walk can be recorded for display in two different ways:

◆ Turn the story of the walk into a book, using a similar format to *Rosie's Walk*: 'Mrs Andrew, Shauna, Conor and Dev went for a walk around the chairs, across the mats, past the tables, through the kitchen .... and got back to the book corner in time for story.' Ask the children to make pictures for each area and set out the story so that you have one place/position word per page: *around the chairs* with a picture on one page, *across the mats* with a picture on the next page. Involve the children in cutting and sticking the pages of the book and ask any writers to help with writing the story. Finish off with the ending - 'and got back to the book corner in time for story.' Think of a title to write on the front cover of your book - *Shauna, Conor and Dev's Walk.*

◆ Make a map of your walk. (See 'A map of Rosie's farmyard' activity and follow the same process.)

Encourage the children to use their book or map to retrace their walk, taking other children along with them. Older children could try using each other's maps or books as a guide so that they can follow the same walk.

ASSESSMENT

How involved is each child in planning the walk with the group? Does she interpret the position words correctly or does she need to be guided by the adult? Take into account age and whether English is a first language in assessing the child's understanding of position words.

EARLY LEARNING GOALS

Knowledge and Understanding of the World:
Observe, find out about and identify features in the place they live and the natural world.
Mathematical Development:
Use everyday words to describe position.
Physical Development:
Move with control and co-ordination.
Travel around, under, over and through balancing and climbing equipment.
Show awareness of space, of themselves and of others.
Move with confidence, imagination and in safety.
Communication, Language and Literacy:
Interact with others, negotiating plans and activities.

ACTIVITY - *A map of Rosie's farmyard*

ABOUT THE ACTIVITY

This activity involves making a map of Rosie's farmyard and marking the route she takes on her walk.

Each page of the book shows Rosie strolling through a different part of the farmyard. On openings 5 and 6 she is walking across the yard; on openings 7 and 8 she is strolling around the pond. The different parts are shown separately on the pages of the book, but they can all be added together to create a complete picture of the farmyard. On the title page of the book (opening 2), there is a small picture of the whole farmyard, showing the different parts that Rosie walks around.

Making a map of Rosie's farmyard helps the children gain a sense of the entire setting for the story. It also introduces the skill of map making. Tracing and marking Rosie's route on the map introduces orienteering skills and helps the children to understand the meaning of the different position words: *across, around, over, past, through* and *under.*

GROUP

Up to six children.

WHAT YOU WILL NEED

Rosie's Walk
Drawing paper and pencils
Scissors and glue
Backing paper

WHAT TO DO

Read through *Rosie's Walk* with the children and then look at the picture on the title page. Explain that this picture shows all the different parts of the farmyard. Find some of the landmarks from the story to compare with the title page picture - the pond and the weeping willow on openings 7 and 8; the beehives on openings 13, 14 and 15.

Ask the children to draw pictures of the different landmarks - the yard, the pond, the haycock, the mill, the fence, the beehives and Rosie's coop. Look at and talk about the pictures in the story, to ensure that the children understand what they are drawing.
Cut out the pictures and place them on the large piece of paper in a rough circle so that the yard (the first destination) is on one side of the hen coop and the beehives (the last destination) are on the other side. Glue them on. The map is now ready for you to trace Rosie's journey. Choose a brightly coloured pen or pencil. Look at the first part of the story: 'Rosie the hen went for a walk across the yard ...' Encourage the child to trace a route from the hen coop across the yard with her finger and then draw it in with the pencil. Look at the second part of the story - 'around the pond ...' Ask a second child to trace the route, making it clear what is meant by 'around'. She can then draw it in. Continue until the route is completed and Rosie is back at the hen coop in time for dinner.

MAKE A DISPLAY
Plan a written explanation of the map, making a note of their suggestions. This can then be turned into a heading and the map can be pinned to the wall. If possible, place copies of *Rosie's Walk* on a table beneath the map.

ASSESSMENT
Is the child able to draw her own pictures of Rosie's farmyard? Is she able to use the position words to trace Rosie's route on the map or does she need a lot of help? Take into account age and whether English is the child's first language when assessing her understanding of position words.

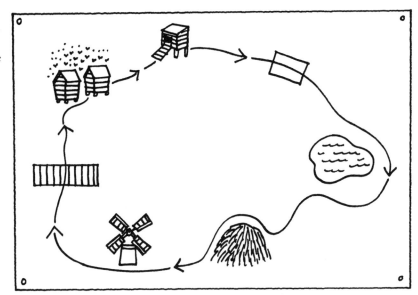

EARLY LEARNING GOALS
Knowledge and Understanding of the World:
Observe, find out about and identify features in the place they live and the natural world.
Mathematical Development:
Use everyday words to describe position.

Communication, Language and Literacy:
Interact with others, negotiating plans and activities ...
Creative Development:
Explore colour, texture, shape, form and space in two or three dimensions.

ACTIVITY- *Looking at trees*

ABOUT THE ACTIVITY
Pat Hutchins uses lots of strong line and pattern in the pictures for *Rosie's Walk*. The pictures are not naturalistic in that you would never find a real tree looking like the ones in the story. They do, however, show the child how things are structured. For example, the pattern on Rosie's tail feathers shows us how a feather is made up; the nest in the tree on opening 4 shows us how a nest rests in the crook made by two branches of a tree. The pictures clearly show the pattern of bricks on a wall, tiles on a roof, grain on a wooden fence.

The pictures can be used as a starting point for looking at the patterns and structures of leaves and trees. The trees in the book show how branches join to the trunk, how twigs join to the branches, the different ways in which leaves join to twigs and the pattern of veins on the leaves themselves.

GROUPS
A nature walk - dependent on the age of the children and the number of available helpers.
Looking and talking - about six children.
Recording your walk - four children at a time.

WHAT YOU WILL NEED
A nature walk - bags or baskets to gather fallen leaves and twigs.
Looking and talking - *Rosie's Walk*; twigs and plants with leaves attached; a variety of different leaves; a piece of bark; magnifying glasses.
Drawing and making - drawing paper, preferably white cartridge paper; drawing pencils, preferably grade B for older children; paper; green and brown wax crayons and tape for bark and leaf rubbings; green paint for leaf prints; twigs.

WHAT TO DO
◆ **A NATURE WALK:** Start off with a nature walk in the park or the garden. Enlist as many adult helpers as you can and discuss with them what you are looking out for. Encourage the children to look at bushes and trees,

focusing in particular on the different ways in which the leaves are attached to the twigs. Look also at the patterns of veins on the leaves. Gather any fallen leaves and twigs to bring back with you. Check first if you are in a park or other public place as it can be illegal to remove anything

from the area. Discuss with the children beforehand the importance of not removing leaves or twigs directly from the trees.

Introduce a variety of language, asking your helpers to do so as well: twig, branch, trunk, leaf, vein, pattern, join, stalk; also any appropriate describing words such as rough, smooth, crinkly, knobbly.

◆ **LOOKING AND TALKING:** Once back in your setting, gather the children in a group and look at the structure of the trees in *Rosie's Walk*. Openings 5, 6 and 7 all have clear pictures of trees.

Look at examples of real twigs and plants you have gathered, showing the leaves attached in different patterns. Show the children that some leaves have long stalks, others have short stalks, some are joined on either side of the twig opposite each other, while others are adjacent. Show the children the single leaf at the end of some twigs.

Look at the pattern of veins on the leaves in *Rosie's Walk* and then show the children the patterns on the real leaves. If you have older ones in your group, you can explain why the veins are there. Discuss the similarities and differences between the different types of leaves you have gathered.

Show the children the pattern of bark on the trees in *Rosie's Walk*. Look at and feel the texture of the piece of bark. Look at any of the twigs large enough to have a covering of bark.

Use a magnifying glass to look at leaf veins and bark patterns. Talk about what difference the magnifying glass makes.

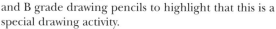

◆ **DRAWING AND MAKING:** Ask those children who are able to do representational drawings to look carefully at the twigs and leaves and then draw them. If possible, give the children proper drawing paper (white cartridge paper) and B grade drawing pencils to highlight that this is a special drawing activity.

Tape paper over the piece of bark or, better still, on to the trunk of a tree in the garden. Using the side of a brown wax crayon, show the children how to take rubbings of the bark. Discuss the pattern you have made. Place paper over the leaves and take rubbings with a green wax crayon. Choose a leaf with strong veins and a long stem. Paint it with green paint and then make a leaf print by pressing it down on a piece of paper, holding it firmly and then lifting it off by its stem. Discuss the patterns you have made.

MAKE A DISPLAY

Cut out the bark rubbings to make collage pieces. These can then be glued onto the outline of a tree, drawn on a large piece of paper. The leaf rubbings and prints can be cut out and stuck on to the twigs of your tree. You can also add real leaves and cut-out paintings of leaves. Look again at the pictures in *Rosie's Walk* and the twigs you have collected and discuss where on the twigs and branches your leaves should be stuck, and the pattern you are going to follow. Involve the children with cutting and gluing, as well as deciding where on the tree the leaves should be glued.

Tie cut-out leaves onto real twigs and place in a jam jar.

You could add large labels to your tree, naming the different parts: trunk, branch, twig, leaf, stalk, vein. Ask any writers in the group to help with labels.

ASSESSMENT

A nature walk: how widely does the child explore her environment on the walk? How closely is she able to follow instructions and how does she conduct herself in the environment beyond the setting? What discoveries does she make?

Looking and talking: how closely does the child observe the items that have been collected? Is she able to use all her senses to explore the twigs, leaves and bark? What

contribution does she make to the discussion with questions and comments? Look out also for signs that the child has absorbed and is starting to use some of the new words you have introduced.

Drawing and making: look out for how adept the older child is with her pencil and how closely she can observe details and reproduce them in her drawings. How easily can she control her movements and the materials to make bark rubbings? How well does she handle printing with leaves? (see Assessment for 'Printing handkerchiefs', page 28).

EARLY LEARNING GOALS
Personal, Social and Emotional Development:
Be confident to try new activities.
Communication, Language and Literacy:
Interact with others, negotiating plans and activities and taking turns in conversation.
Sustain attentive listening, responding to what they have heard by relevant comments, questions or actions.

Extend their vocabulary, exploring the meaning and sounds of new words.
Knowledge and Understanding of the World:
Observe, find out about and identify features in the place they live and the natural world.
Find out about their environment, and talk about those features they like and dislike.
Investigate objects and materials by using all of their senses as appropriate.
Look closely at similarities, differences, pattern and change.
Ask questions about why things happen and how things work.
Creative Development:
Explore colour, texture, shape, form and space in two or three dimensions.
Mathematical Development:
Talk about, recognise and recreate simple patterns.

FIVE-MINUTE ACTIVITIES

HUNT FOR ROSIE
Make a 'Rosie' from stiff card or use the template on page 89. Select one position word and find a hiding place for Rosie that corresponds with your chosen word - behind the books in the book corner or behind the pencils pots. Challenge one or two children to hunt for Rosie, giving them a clue that uses the position word - 'Can you find Rosie behind the books in the book corner?' Emphasise the position word and make sure that Rosie is visible so that the child can spot her, even if she doesn't know the word. Choose other hiding places and position words for later games - under the chairs; beside the mats; above the cooker in the home corner.

If you want to play the game with a larger number of children, make and hide more than one Rosie at a time. Continue the game by planning hiding places in advance and asking a helper to re-hide the cut-outs while you keep the children occupied.

BE AN EGG
Show the children how to act out the three main stages in the life-cycle of the hen: curl up into a tiny ball (egg); wriggle on the floor and make cheeping sounds (chick); strut about

flapping wings and clucking (hen). Play music for the children to dance to. When the music stops, name one of the stages for the children to perform. Re-start the music as a sign to end the action and begin dancing again. If necessary, ask a helper to join in, to remind the children of the different actions.

HENS AND EGGS
Rosie's Walk can be used as the starting point for looking at the life-cycle of a hen.

Look at the pictures of Rosie and point out her feathers, tail, claws, beak and so on. Look at where she lives - her hencoop in the farmyard. Lead on to a discussion about the life-cycle of the hen - laying an egg, the chick hatching and growing into a hen. Talk about eggs and how we use them. Use the templates on page 89.

For a display, make a circular chart showing the life-cycle, following the same process as the 'Life-cycle of a butterfly' (see page 52).

UNDER THE TREE
Have a farmyard model of a hen and other animals, such as a cow, sheep, pig, tree, farmer.

With a small group of children, ask them to put Rosie in different positions, using appropriate words - 'Put Rosie behind the cow'; 'Put Rosie next to the pig'.

Have fun - 'Put Rosie under the tree ...... Put the tree under Rosie!'

When the children are ready, ask them to give you instructions for positioning Rosie.

About Ten, Nine, Eight

A counting book that has remained in print for nearly 20 years has to be special - and *Ten, Nine, Eight* **certainly is.**

The book centres around an Afro-Caribbean father helping his little girl get ready for bed. In 1982, when the book was first published, it was not easy to find stories featuring characters from ethnic minorities or father/child relationships. Even today, with so many more choices available, it remains an outstanding example of its kind.

The format is simple, with the domestic setting providing various items to count. These are described in the gentle rhyming text *(10 small toes all washed and warm, 9 soft friends in a quiet room ...)* and at the same time depicted in the colourful paintings. This combination of words, printed symbols and pictures enables the child to hear the name of the quantity as the book is read aloud (one, two, three), see the symbol in writing (1, 2, 3) and look at and count the objects - ten toes, nine toys, eight window panes and so on.

ACTIVITY - *Body counting*

ABOUT THE ACTIVITY
Many of the counting items in *Ten, Nine, Eight* are connected to the child or her father: ten toes, five buttons, four eyes (the child's and the father's), three kisses on cheeks and nose, two strong arms and one big girl all ready for bed. This can be used as the starting point for counting body parts with the children in your group.

'The body' makes a good counting frame for young children. The different parts are familiar and all the children can count together as they each have the same set. It can also be done on the spur of the moment, without having to gather and set out equipment. The body naturally introduces the child to the most significant number groups within the decimal system - two, five and ten.

GROUP
Any reasonable size for counting body parts; as small as possible for making body shapes.

WHAT YOU WILL NEED
Ten, Nine, Eight
Large sheets of paper, such as the back of a wallpaper roll (make sure it is not ready pasted)
A marker pen or thick pencil for drawing outlines
Labels with 1, 2, 3, 4, 5, and 6, 7, 8, 9, 10 for older children
Buttons, ribbons, wool and other collage materials
Painting and drawing materials
Scissors and glue

WHAT TO DO
Start off by reading through *Ten, Nine, Eight*. Whenever a body part is counted, encourage the children to count their own toes, eyes, buttons and so on.

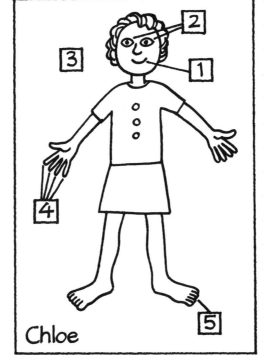

Chloe

Counting up to five: it is easy to find body parts for one to five. Try counting one mouth, nose, head, tummy; two eyes, ears, eyebrows, hands, feet; borrow three kisses on cheeks and nose from *Ten, Nine, Eight* for three; count the fingers on one hand or arms and legs for four; count the toes on one foot for five.

Counting up to ten and beyond: using the body as a means of counting beyond five takes a little more imagination. The hands, eyes or ears of three or four children will give you six or eight items to count; you can count the heads of seven or nine children while ten is easily counted using fingers and thumbs or toes.

You can also count freckles, beads, buttons, the spots on a jumper, the eyelets on shoes with laces, the number of pony tails or hair bands in a group. Encourage the children to count with you and choose their own body parts or items to count.

Along with numbers one to ten, you can introduce other language to do with quantity: a pair, couple, lots of, many, more than, less than, fewer.

MAKE A DISPLAY
Ask the children to lie down on a large piece of paper and draw round their bodies. Make sure their arms are positioned away from their bodies with fingers spread out. Write each child's name on his or her outline.

Show the children how to draw or paint facial details, or stick on collage pieces. If you wish to extend the activity, they can also decorate their bodies using painting, printing and collage. Show the children the labels with 1, 2, 3, 4 and 5 and help them to choose features representing each quantity. Use a felt-pen and draw lines from the chosen features to the edge of the paper. Show each child how to stick the number label at the end of the line (see illustration).

For older children who are ready, you can also add numbers from six to ten. Give the children a selection of buttons and ribbons. Help them to count out different quantities and stick them onto their picture. They can also create quantities by adding freckles with a felt pen, sticking on separate strands of wool to represent hair and drawing in their toes to make ten.

Display your people on the wall. Ask the children to help you decide on a heading, such as 'We have found lots of things to count on our bodies'. Look at the outlines with the children and count the different body parts on a regular basis, to help consolidate the children's counting skills.

ASSESSMENT

Look out for the child's ability to count each quantity. Can she count in sequence? When making body shapes, is the child able to match each quantity with its symbol? Look out for how the child handles glue and scissors (see Assessment for 'Animal flaps', page 30).

EARLY LEARNING GOALS

Mathematical Development:
Say and use number names in order in familiar contexts.
Count reliably up to 10 everyday objects.
Recognise numerals 1 to 9.
In practical activities and discussion begin to use the vocabulary involved in adding and subtracting.
Find one more or one less than a number from one to 10.
Physical Development:
Handle tools, objects, construction and malleable materials safely and with increasing control.
Show awareness of ... themselves and others.
Creative Development:
Explore colour, texture, shape, form and space in two or three dimensions.

A C T I V I T Y - *Toys*

ABOUT THE ACTIVITY

The setting for *Ten, Nine, Eight* is the little girl's bedroom containing all her toys. The soft toys in her collection make up the counting group for number nine - *9 soft friends in a quiet room.* Throughout the book, other toys are featured in the pictures, making it a useful starting point for looking at toys with your group. The activities below focus on sorting toys according to different criteria (material, type, purpose), talking about and displaying a favourite toy and exploring toys from the past.

GROUP

Any reasonable size for looking at old toys; as small as possible for sorting activities and talking about favourite toys.

WHAT YOU WILL NEED

Ten, Nine, Eight
A favourite toy belonging to each child
A collection of toys to suit various sorting criteria
Toys from the past (ask parents and grandparents)
Hoops or mats for sorting
Clip-board and marker pen for taking notes
Drawing materials
Papers for mounting and display

WHAT TO DO

◆ **MY FAVOURITE TOY:** look at the toys in *Ten, Nine, Eight.* Encourage the children to talk about their own toys. Do they have toys similar to those in the picture? What is their favourite toy? What do they do with their different toys?
Send a note home, asking for a favourite toy to be brought in from home (preferably unbreakable and something that is not crucial to the child's bedtime

routine!) Working in small groups, talk to each child about her toy - what it looks like, what it is made of, how you play with it, how long the child has had it, where it came from, why it is special and so on. Make notes of what the child has to say. Ask the children to look carefully at their toys and draw them. You could also take photographs.

◆ **TOYS FROM THE PAST:** toys make useful artefacts through which to get children exploring the past. Send a note home asking for parents, grandparents and even teenagers to lend one of their toys to your group. Emphasise to the children that the toys must be handled carefully, partly because they are old and partly because they belong to somebody else. While the pre-school child will not have much sense of her own immediate past, you can still make a start at introducing an historical context by explaining that a doll or teddy bear belonged to grandma when she was little. Wherever possible, compare a modern version with the old toy. Point out the differences and similarities - in particular, the features that show the old toy is old (metal not plastic, threadbare, battered and worn, softer colours, no micro chips, batteries or devices that are found in the toys of today).

Many museums run a loan service and will lend genuine historical artefacts to schools. Invite a grandparent or great grandparent into your setting to talk to the children about the toys and games they played with when they were little.

◆ **SORTING TOYS:** sort into hoops or mats, choosing criteria to match the age, ability and experience of your children:

Ten, Nine, Eight

- ◆ **Colour:** toys of different types but falling into two or three colour categories.
- ◆ **Different types within a category:** soft toys - teddies, rabbits, dogs; construction - Stickle bricks, Duplo, Lego.
- ◆ **Type of toy:** toy vehicles, cuddly toys, jigsaws.
- ◆ **Purpose:** construction toys (Duplo, Stickle bricks, wooden blocks), water toys, kitchen toys (tea sets, rolling pins).
- ◆ **Opinion:** toys a child likes/does not like.
- ◆ **Toys for different ages:** babies - rattles, teething rings, rag books; older children - jigsaws, Lego, toy crane.
- ◆ **Old and new:** toys from when mummy and granny were little; toys from today.
- ◆ **Material:** wooden, plastic, metal.

MAKE A DISPLAY

My favourite toy: write out what the child has said about her toy or ask any children who are ready to write some words about their toy. Display the writing along with her drawing of the toy and, if possible, the toy itself. Add a heading: 'These are our favourite toys'.

Toys from the past: display the old toys that you have managed to collect. If possible, add pictures of children from the same era as the toy. Explain to the children that these toys must not be touched.

Sorting toys: ask the children to draw pictures of the toys they have sorted. Alternatively, go through an old toy catalogue and cut out pictures. These can then be stuck onto two circles of paper according to the criteria you are using, and displayed on the wall with appropriate headings.

ASSESSMENT

How much does each child contribute to the discussion? Is she able to tailor her contribution to the topic of toys? Look out for how fluently and confidently she expresses herself, the complexity of her sentences and the range of vocabulary she uses.

Look out for signs that older children are developing a sense of the past through understanding that a toy belonged to grandma when she was little.

When sorting toys, are the children able to use the agreed criteria to put the toys into their groups? Make sure that you choose criteria suitable to the child's age.

EARLY LEARNING GOALS
Knowledge and Understanding of the World:
Investigate objects and materials by using all of their senses as appropriate.
Observe, find out about and identify features in the place they live and the natural world.
Look closely at similarities, differences, patterns and change.
Ask questions about why things happen and how things work.
Find out about past and present events in their own lives, and in those of other people they know.
Communication, Language and Literacy:
Enjoy listening to and using spoken and written language, and readily turn to it in their play and learning.
Sustain attentive listening, responding to what they have heard by relevant comments, questions or actions.
Extend their vocabulary.
Physical Development:
Handle tools, objects, construction and malleable materials safely and with increasing control.

A C T I V I T Y - *Night and day*

ABOUT THE ACTIVITY

Ten, Night, Eight revolves around the aspect of night that is most obvious to the young child - bedtime. This can be a good moment to get the children thinking about some other features of night time and day time. They can then go on to use their knowledge of night and day time characteristics to make night and day carousels (see below).

GROUP

Any reasonable size for talking about night time and day time; keep as small as possible for making the carousels.

WHAT YOU WILL NEED

Ten, Night, Eight
Circles cut from card, one pair for each child
Brass paper-fasteners
Scissors
Paint or sugar paper in pale blue and dark blue
Silver, gold and white paper for stars, moon, sun and clouds
Magazine pictures of day time and night time things
Glue

WHAT TO DO

Talking about night and day: focus on the aspects of *Ten, Night, Eight* that link with night time - wearing a night gown (opening 10), sleepy eyes (opening 11), window panes showing the night sky (opening 7).

Discuss other features and characteristics of night time, comparing it with day time. Let the children lead the discussion with what they know and understand about night time. You can also introduce elements such as:
- ◆ going to bed and sleeping
- ◆ darkness, moon and stars
- ◆ putting on lights - street lights, car headlights, torches, lights in the house
- ◆ changes in temperature
- ◆ nocturnal animals

Making night and day carousels: give each child two card circles. Divide one (circle 1) in half with a straight line. Cut a window into half of the other (circle 2). Colour the two halves of circle 1 so that one half is dark blue, to represent a night-time sky and the other pale blue to represent a day-time sky.

This can be done with paint or sponge printing, or by sticking on semi-circles of coloured sugar paper.
Help the children to choose what to put on the dark blue and the light blue backgrounds to make night-time and day-time pictures. Some possibilities include:

◆ **night time -** moon, stars, owl, cat, streetlight
◆ **day time -** sun, clouds, children playing, dogs
Older children can draw and cut out pictures or shapes from coloured paper. Provide younger ones with ready-cut shapes such as stars, moons, suns and clouds. You can also give them magazine pictures.

Cut out a window

Circle 1   Circle 2

Once circle 1 has been completed, you can attach circle 2. Join the two circles at the centre with a brass paper-fastener so that circle 2 is on top of circle 1 (see illustration). Make sure that the circles are joined loosely so that the top circle will revolve easily. Holding the top circle, show the children how to turn the bottom circle so that the picture revealed in the window changes from day, to night, to day, to night ...
The children can either decorate circle 2 or leave it plain.
Older children could write something to stick on to circle 2.

MAKE A DISPLAY

Put up a large sheet of dark blue paper decorated with cut-out silver stars and a moon, and a large sheet of pale blue paper with a sun and clouds. Pin half the carousels showing their night pictures to the dark paper and the other half showing their day pictures to the light paper. Encourage the children to help you think of a heading.

ASSESSMENT

Talking about night and day: is the child able to use her knowledge and experience of night and day to contribute to the discussion? Look out for how fluently and confidently she expresses herself, the complexity of her sentences and the range of vocabulary she uses.
Making night and day carousels: look out for how accurately the children are able to choose symbols to stick on the two halves of the carousel. How do they handle scissors and glue? (see Assessment for 'Animal flaps', page 30).

EARLY LEARNING GOALS
Knowledge and Understanding of the World:
Observe, find out about and identify features in the place they live and the natural world.
Look closely at similarities, differences, patterns and change
Ask questions about why things happen and how things work.
Select the tools and techniques they need to shape, assemble and join materials they are using.
Communication, Language and Literacy:
Enjoy listening to and using spoken and written language, and readily turn to it in their play and learning.
Sustain attentive listening, responding to what they have heard by relevant comments, questions or actions.
Creative Development:
Explore colour, texture, shape, form and space in two or three dimensions.
Use their imagination in art and design.
Express and communicate their ideas, thoughts and feelings by using a widening range of materials, suitable tools ... designing and making.
Physical Development:
Handle tools, objects, construction and malleable materials safely and with increasing control.

FIVE-MINUTE ACTIVITIES

BEDTIME STORIES
Read some other stories with night-time themes, such as Martin Waddell's *Owl Babies* (Walker), *The Walker Book of Bedtime Stories* (Walker), Jill Murphy's *A Quiet Night In* (Walker), Niki Daly and Louis Baum's *I Want to See the Moon* (Red Fox), Margaret Wise Brown's classic *Goodnight Moon* (Mammoth) and for something unusual, Bruce Ingman's *A Night on the Tiles*

(Mammoth). Get your children to retell these stories or make up their own. Record them and then put the tapes and the tape recorder in the 'bedroom corner' for children to listen to.

MATCHING NUMBERS
This is an activity for children who can count and recognise numbers. Make two sets of cards, one set with pictures of quantities (ten toes, nine toys, eight

window panes) and one set with matching symbols (10, 9, 8). Use the items from *Ten, Nine, Eight* if you want to link the activity with the book, or any other items if you prefer. Give each child a picture card and help them to match the quantities with their number symbols. Make it easy or difficult by varying the number of symbol cards for the child to choose from.

About The Nursery Collection

The Nursery Collection brings together a range of concept books that were first published separately.

The collection is made up of the following:
- *Bathwater's Hot* (opposites and contrasts)
- *All Shapes and Sizes*

- *When We Went to the Park* (number from one to ten)
- *Colours*
- *Noisy* (different sounds)

Each book presents its concept through the everyday adventures of a little girl and her baby brother. Shirley Hughes is one of the best illustrators

around and this book is a delight from start to finish. Beautifully painted pictures feature all kinds of familiar scenes as the little girl helps tidy up, goes for a walk with grandad in the park, or picnics with her mother and baby brother. With so many different concepts to explore, this book offers something for all ages.

A C T I V I T Y - *Environmental qualities*

ABOUT THE ACTIVITY

This activity links with *Bathwater's Hot* and *All Shapes and Sizes*. It introduces different environmental qualities through contrasting pairs - for example, rough/smooth; hot/cold; soft/hard. Contrast is one of the best ways of highlighting a quality to the young child. Until the child knows from experience that sandpaper feels rough, she will not register it as rough without also being able to compare it with something smooth. As the child feels the two textures, you can introduce the words *rough* and *smooth*.

Gathering the resources for the activity is time consuming, but once they have been prepared, you can use them again and again. The list of pairs below are only suggestions. Add your own ideas, but make sure that each pair of items is similar in some way so that the child can match them before going on to experience the quality.

GROUP
Preferably no more than three.

WHAT YOU WILL NEED
The Nursery Collection
Two pairs of matching plastic bottles
Hot/cold water
Food colouring
Sandpaper; stiff card; marbles; sand; cotton wool
Fabric, needle and thread
A pair of identical empty spice tubs
A pair of identical sponges
Two chime bars
Two pebbles
Fur fabric
Pairs of similar items in large/small and short/tall sizes
Glue
Scissors

WHAT TO DO
Prepare your pairs of items. Wherever possible, make your pairs identical so that the only difference is the quality you want to highlight. Try some of the following:

- **Hot/cold** - fill one plastic bottle with cold water and one with hot.
- **Rough/smooth** - cut out two identical cats' heads from card and glue sandpaper onto one of them. Draw on faces with a black marker pen.
- **Heavy/light** - sew two bean bags (same shape, size and colour) and fill one with marbles and one with cotton wool.
- **Soft/loud** - fill one plastic spice container with marbles and one with sand. Tape the lids on firmly.
- **Full/empty** - fill a plastic bottle with coloured water and put only a small amount of coloured water into an identical bottle.
- **Large/small** - find two similar items in large and small size - teddy bears, books, leaves.
- **Tall or long/short** - find two similar items in tall or long and short sizes - ribbons, pencils, candles.
- **High/low** (notes) - find a chime bar with a high note and a chime bar with a low note.
- **Wet/dry** - dampen one sponge and leave an identical sponge dry.
- **Hard/soft** - glue a piece of fur fabric onto the surface of one pebble and leave the other plain.
- **Light/dark** - find two similar items in a dark shade and a light shade of the same colour.

Once you have prepared your items, read through *Bathwater's Hot* and *All Shapes and Sizes* with the children. Concentrate in particular on the environmental qualities:
- **Opening 6** - *Bathwater's hot, Seawater's cold.*
- **Opening 8** - *Some things are hard as stone, Some are soft as cloud.*
- **Opening 10** - *Night-time is dark, daytime is light.*
- **Opening 25** - *This jar's empty, Now it's full.*

Set out one of each pair on a mat or low table and place the rest in a box. Give a child an item and ask her to choose the item that goes with it. Give her a little help if necessary. Once she has chosen the second item, help her to experience the quality: wrap the whole hand around the water bottles to feel the different temperatures; stroke the cats' heads lightly with the finger tips to feel the different textures; shake the spice jars beside the ear, one at a time to listen to their different volumes.

As the child experiences the different qualities, introduce words to describe them - *rough, smooth; light, heavy; soft, hard.* Let the other children in the group experience the qualities. If you keep the group as small as possible, all the children can have lots of turns.

ASSESSMENT

Look out for whether the child is able to explore the items and experience their quality. Look out for her reactions, both in words and facial expression. This will indicate whether the quality has made an impact on her. Are older children starting to learn the words to describe the different qualities? Give the children plenty of opportunity to repeat their experiences, to help them absorb and use the language.

EARLY LEARNING GOALS

Knowledge and Understanding of the World:
Observe, find out about and identify features in the place

they live and the natural world.
Look closely at similarities, differences, patterns and change.
Communication, Language and Literacy:
Extend their vocabulary.
Creative Development:
Respond in a variety of ways to what they see, hear, smell, touch and feel.
Explore colour, texture, shape, form and space in two or three dimensions.
Physical Development:
Handle tools, objects, construction and malleable materials safely and with increasing control.

ACTIVITY - *Exploring the environment*

ABOUT THE ACTIVITY

The pairs of items in the above activity are simply an introduction to different environmental qualities. Once the children have played with the pairs and you have introduced the words that describe the qualities, you can encourage the children to explore texture, weight, size, sound and so on, in a much wider sense.

GROUP

Preferably no more than three at a time.

WHAT YOU WILL NEED

A kettle; mirror; ice cubes; saucers
Papers with rough and smooth textures (see below)
Backing paper cut into squares
Glue; scissors
A collection of: objects of different weights; soft and hard

objects; small/large and short/tall objects
Two hoops or trays for sorting
A tape recorder; percussion instruments

WHAT TO DO

Try the following activities to broaden the child's exploration of the environment:

◆ **Hot and cold:** take a walk around the setting with a small group, looking for hot and cold items such as the fridge, the radiator, the window pane (hot or cold depending on season), the hot and cold taps in cloakrooms, the adult's tea. Ask the children to make drawings of hot items and cold items to sort and stick onto two cut-out paper circles.

Try some hot and cold water experiments with your older children. Show the children the steam from the boiling kettle (keep the group small and have an adult with the children while somebody else deals with the kettle). Carefully hold a mirror above the steam and show the group what happens. Take ice cubes from the freezer. Put them in two different saucers. Put one in a warm place, such as by the radiator, and another in a cold place, such as in the fridge. Can the children predict what will happen? Place a saucer of water in a warm place and a saucer of water in a cold place. Can the children predict what will happen? Check regularly to see how the water and ice cubes are changing and make drawings of the results to put up on the wall.

◆ **Rough and smooth tiles:** gather a range of different collage materials, representing rough and smooth textures. Rough - sandpaper, corrugated card, paper with pin pricks (place paper on wooden bread board and puncture with a needle), dried flowers, crumpled tissue and silver foil. Smooth - cellophane, card, paper, shiny paper, smooth silver foil. Help the children to sort the materials into rough and smooth and stick them onto square pieces of paper. These can then be pinned to the wall, alternating a rough tile with a smooth tile. Rough and smooth tiles can also be made with clay or Plasticene. Roll out the clay and cut it into tiles with a knife or a biscuit cutter. Use a glue spatula or a pencil to make marks in the clay. Press Lego or Stickle bricks into the surface. Leave some tiles smooth and varnish when dry. Compare the rough and smooth surfaces of the tiles.

◆ **Heavy and light collections:** take a walk around the setting and the garden with a small group of older children and a basket. Choose items to sort into two categories - heavy and light. If possible, stick to items that can be held in one hand. Once you have gathered your items, choose an object of medium weight, such as a small book. This is your control. Show the children how to weigh the control item in one hand and another item in the other hand. If they think the item is heavier than the control, it goes in the heavy section, if it feels lighter, it goes in the light section.

Have some suitable items in mind, as well as letting the children choose their own. Weight is quite a difficult concept for young children to grasp. Start them off with items that are much heavier and much lighter than the control, such as a feather or a large pebble. A sharp

contrast makes it easier for the children to realise that they are testing weight. Some other possibilities could include cotton wool, a leaf, a flannel, a pencil, a wooden block, a stone, a shell, a mug, a paperweight. If you have balance scales in your setting, this will give you a more accurate idea of how each item compares with the control.

Make an interactive display by setting out the heavy and the light items on a table in two boxes or trays. Place the control item on the table with some further items to be sorted. Label the heavy and light section. Change the items to be sorted from time to time and encourage the children to find their own items to add to the display.

◆ **Soft and hard collections:** explore soft and hard in the same ways as light and heavy, looking out for and sorting things in the environment that feel soft or hard. Some possibilities include a cuddly toy, a cushion, a woolly glove, cotton wool, a flannel, playdough; a stone, a book, a tray, a spoon, a building brick, a toy car.

◆ **Loud sounds and soft sounds:** explore some further ways of making loud and soft sounds. Have another look at opening 8, *Whisper very quietly, Shout OUT LOUD!* Try experimenting with quiet voices and loud voices. Try clapping hands or stamping feet gently or firmly to make loud sounds and soft sounds. Show the children the volume button on the tape recorder and how to turn the volume up and down. Get out the percussion instruments and explore making loud and soft sounds.
Read through *Noisy* with the children and gather together some role-play props, such as wooden spoons and saucepans, a toy plane, a telephone. Encourage the

Are these objects heavier than the book or lighter than the book?

heavy

light

children to mimic and create the sounds in the story and talk about whether they are loud or soft, and how they make them feel. With older children you may be able to start looking at the reason behind sounds. Why is a telephone loud? What makes a dog bark or a baby cry?

ASSESSMENT

When searching the environment for different sensory experiences (hot, cold, light, heavy) is the child aware of what she is looking for? How accurately can she follow your instructions to begin with and how much can she discover independently once she understands what she is looking for? How much does she engage in the various experiences you offer and how closely does she observe experiments? Are older children able to predict what will happen?

Look out for whether the child is able to use the different criteria for sorting and making collections and organise the items into their different groups. How does she handle scissors and glue when making 'Rough and smooth tiles'? (see Assessment for 'Animal flaps', page 30).

EARLY LEARNING GOALS

Knowledge and Understanding of the World:
Observe, find out about and identify features in the place they live and the natural world.
Ask questions about why things happen and how things work.
Look closely at similarities, differences, patterns and change.
Communication, Language and Literacy:
Sustain attentive listening, responding to what they have heard by relevant comments, questions or actions.
Extend their vocabulary.
Creative Development:
Respond in a variety of ways to what they see, hear, smell, touch and feel.
Explore colour, texture, shape, form and space in two or three dimensions.
Recognise and explore how sounds can be changed.
Physical Development:
Handle tools, objects, construction and malleable materials safely and with increasing control.
Move with control and co-ordination.
Show awareness of space, of themselves and of others.

ACTIVITY - *Movement opposites*

ABOUT THE ACTIVITY
These activities are all based on contrasting actions, behaviours and positions.

GROUP
Up to six children.

WHAT YOU WILL NEED
The Nursery Collection
Various props for role play including a waste-paper bin, a toy car, a slide, a large box, a chair (see below).

WHAT TO DO
Actions and behaviours: read through *Bathwater's Hot* and *All Shapes and Sizes*. Focus in particular on the opposites and contrasts that involve action:
◆ **Opening 7** - *Some things you can throw away, Some are nice to keep, Here's someone who is wide awake... Shhh, he's fast asleep.*
◆ **Opening 8** - *Whisper very quietly, Shout OUT LOUD!* and *It's fun to run very fast, Or to be slow.*
◆ **Opening 9** - *It's kind to be helpful, Unkind to tease, Rather rude to push and grab, Polite to say 'please'.*
◆ **Opening 24** - *Climb up the ladder, Slip down the slide.*
◆ **Opening 25** - *Get behind to push, Get in front to pull.*

Invite children to role play the different actions - throwing something in the waste-paper bin/putting something away carefully in a drawer; being asleep/being wide awake; whispering/shouting; running/walking slowly; being kind and helpful/being unkind; being rude/being polite (discuss with the children a possible scenario to illustrate these behaviours); climbing up the slide/slipping down the slide (save for the garden); pushing a toy car/pulling a toy car.

As the children become able to recognise the opposites and contrasts, whisper to a child an action to perform and then ask the rest of the group to guess the action. Can one of them come and perform the contrasting or opposite action? Add any other movement contrasts you can think of - stamping/tiptoeing; laughing/crying; jiggling arms, legs, hands and head/keeping very still.

Positions: these activities introduce the child to contrasting positions through movements - up/down; in/out; on top of/below and so on.

Start off by looking at the pages of *All Shapes and Sizes* which focus on position words:

◆ **Opening 22** - *High is far up in the sky, Low is near the ground*
◆ **Opening 23** - *Big Teddy's out, Little Teddy's in*
◆ **Opening 24** - *Climb up the ladder, Slip down the slide*
◆ **Opening 25** - *Get behind to push, Get in front to pull.*

Take a small group of children to the climbing frame. Find different ways of getting into the various positions. Have some children climbing *high up* to the top and some staying *low down* on the ground; have one child *in* the climbing frame and another *out*; position some children *in front* of the frame and others hiding *behind* it; position two children, one *above* and the other *below*. If you have a swing and a slide, make use of them for *up* and *down*, *high* and *low*. Give all the children as many turns as possible to help them learn the different positions and their opposites.

You can also use toys or models and give the children instructions - *put teddy in the car / take teddy out of the car; put teddy under the car / put teddy on top of the car; put teddy behind the car / put teddy in front of the car.*

Once the children know the position words and their contrasts, ask a child to get into a position and invite another child to come and do the opposite position.

ASSESSMENT

Actions and behaviours: assess how the child performs in role play (see 'Grandpa's Handkerchief role play', page 26). Take into account age, previous experience of role-play activities and whether English is the child's first language.

Positions: look out for how adept the child is at getting into the different positions. The degree of prompting she needs will indicate how much she understands the meaning of the position word.

EARLY LEARNING GOALS
◆ **Actions and behaviours:**
Personal, Social and Emotional Development:
Understand what is right, what is wrong and why.
Consider the consequences of their words and actions, for themselves and others.
Communication, Language and Literacy:
Use language to imagine and recreate roles and experiences.

Creative Development:
Use their imagination in role play.
Express and communicate their ideas, thoughts and feelings by using a widening range of materials, suitable tools, imaginative and role play ...
Knowledge and Understanding of the World:
Find out about, and identify, some features of living things, objects and events they observe.

◆ **Positions:**
Physical Development:
Move with control and co-ordination.
Travel around, under, over and through balancing and climbing equipment.
Show awareness of space, of themselves and of others.
Use a range of small and large equipment.
Mathematical Development:
Use everyday words to describe position.

Both activities:
Knowledge and Understanding of the World:
Look closely at similarities, differences, patterns and change
Communication, Language and Literacy:
Extend their vocabulary
Physical Development:
Move with confidence, imagination and in safety.

FIVE-MINUTE ACTIVITIES

THE CONTRASTS RHYME

Try the following poem with your group, getting them to perform the actions as you go along. If you usually have a circle of chairs, make sure the children don't collide with their chairs when they jump back. The change of movement is quite speedy, particularly for little ones. Take the rhyme slowly to begin with :

I'm as tall as the trees (stand up straight)
Now I'm short, down on my knees (kneel or lean down to touch knees)
I can stretch from side to side (stretch out arms as far as they will go)
Which will make me very wide
I'm as big as a house (make yourself as big as possible)
Now I'm small as a mouse (curl up in a ball)
I'm as tall as the trees (stretch up)

I can reach up high (reach up)
I'm a bird and I can fly (flap arms)
I can stoop down low (touch the floor)

I can wiggle to and fro (wiggle from side to side)
I jump forwards, I jump back (jump forwards and backwards)
I jump in and out like that
I can reach up high

COLOUR SORTING

Colours in *The Nursery Collection* can be used as the starting point for 'Colour sorting with objects'. (See *Grandpa's Handkerchief*, page 26).

NUMBER SEQUENCE

When We Went to the Park in *The Nursery Collection* can be used as the starting point for 'Making a number sequence'. Use the same format as for *Washing Line* (page 47). If you have lots of prolific artists in your group, you can ask the children to draw one black cat, two big girls licking ice creams, three ladies, four babies, five children, six runners, seven dogs,

eight footballing boys, nine ducks, ten birds and a great pile of leaves. Alternatively, you can find pictures in magazines and catalogues to cut out, or photocopy your own drawings and make this a colouring, cutting and sticking exercise as well as a counting activity.

SOUNDS TAPE

Make a tape recording of different noises for the children to guess from sound alone. Try some of the following - a piano playing, a toilet flushing, someone clapping, someone laughing, a car engine, a well-known television theme tune. You could also put out objects or pictures for the children to match with the sounds. Play a sound and ask a child to come and choose the object that goes with it. For example, a toy piano from the dolls' house, a toilet roll, a picture of clapping hands, a model car.

About Dear Daddy

Dear Daddy **is a good example of how words and pictures can be used to present quite complex themes and ideas. The story in words takes the form of a simple letter from Sophie to her daddy, who is away at sea. The accompanying pictures are more complex and detailed.**

Author/illustrator Philippe Dupasquier has divided the page into two parts. The lower part consists of Sophie, her mother and baby brother going about their daily business in the family home. The upper part shows Sophie's daddy working aboard a freighter on the other side of the world. The juxtaposition of the two pictures neatly demonstrates that time passes for Sophie and her father concurrently, even though they are separated from each other. As Sophie builds a snowman in the garden with her brother, her daddy is on a beach in the hot sunshine or wandering through a Chinese market looking for presents for Sophie. While Sophie plays in the garden, her dad is hard at work painting the ship. The book ends with the two separate pictures mirroring each other as Sophie and her daddy are reunited at last.

Sophie picks out certain elements of her life to write about in her letter, while the pictures tell their own, more extensive story. Like so many of the best picture books, the pictures add the kind of detail that would be too much to explain in words for the young child - including incidents that directly involve Sophie and incidents that are peripheral to her own little sphere. As an ever-changing backdrop, the pictures reflect the four seasons as the year progresses, until Sophie's daddy finally returns home in a blaze of summer sunshine.

A C T I V I T Y - *Reading Dear Daddy*

ABOUT THE ACTIVITY

Dear Daddy offers so much to look at, think about and discuss, it is well worth setting aside time to share it with just two or three children. A small group enables each child to question and discuss the book as much as she wishes. Try to keep the timing of the sessions open-ended so that you and the children can let your conversation develop naturally and last for as long as necessary. When you hold a small story group with a book such as *Dear Daddy*, you can never predict what will come up, what you and the group will talk about and how the children will interpret the story. Be ready to follow the child's lead and simply answer questions as carefully as possible.

GROUP

Keep as small as possible.

WHAT TO DO

Gather the children around you. If you can keep the group to two or three children, they will be able to sit beside you and look at the pictures as you read. Give the children as much time as they need to study the pictures before turning the pages.

Resist the temptation to refer to the top picture, showing Sophie's daddy and his different life aboard ship. Wait to see if the children comment on it, or whether they give it a different meaning from the one intended by the author. This can tell you a lot about the child's ability to interpret story and pictures. While you can certainly ask questions about the pictures and story if you wish, you will often get more extended conversation with the children if you leave them to comment on what attracts their attention. Let them lead the conversation as much as possible. Don't be concerned if they do not say much on the first reading; if you are able to share the book with the same group a second time, the questions and comments usually start to come thick and fast.

An open-ended session where you allow discussion to develop can last for ages, particularly if you have talkative children. If you find you are running out of time, read through the last few pages quickly. Do try always to finish off the story. This adds a sense of 'wholeness' to the activity and, in the case of *Dear Daddy*, reassures the children that Sophie and her daddy are reunited at last.

The following examples cover elements in the book that can lead to interesting questions, comments and the kind of conversation from which young children can learn so much:

◆ **Events in the picture:** with detailed pictures such as these, it is always fascinating to see what the children notice and how they match the story with the pictures. On opening 5, one of the events taking place in the foreground of the picture is the dustbin men emptying bins into their lorry. There is no mention of the scene in the text so that the picture tells a little story completely extraneous to the main narrative. If you give the children time, they will notice and comment on details such as this. The ensuing conversation offers all kinds of learning opportunities - from the chance for the child to express herself aloud to the interesting information you can offer about dustmen. What is more, you can guarantee the child will be interested because she has raised the topic herself.

◆ **Events in the text:** the opposite situation can also be a useful starting point for conversation - where Sophie refers to something in her letter that is not shown in the picture. On opening 7, Sophie writes to her daddy: 'Timmy and I made a huge snowman'. The picture gives a straightforward representation of this event, showing

Dear Daddy

Sophie and Timmy working on their snowman. However, she goes on to write: 'Mummy says if I'm good, Father Christmas might bring me a bicycle'. There is nothing in the picture that matches these words - no bicycle, no Father Christmas, no picture of Sophie being good. Part of learning to follow a story involves being able to envisage the pictures created by the words, without an illustration to set it all out for you. *Dear Daddy* gives the children lots of opportunity to do this because the pictures and the words so often focus on different things. If a detail or an event that is not depicted catches the child's attention, it shows you that she is listening to the words as well as looking at the pictures.

◆ **Pictorial symbols:** Philippe Dupasquier has a cartoon-like style of illustration and uses little pictorial symbols to show certain things. For example, the autumn leaves on opening 5 have curly lines following them, to represent their fluttering movement as they fall. Until the child has learnt the meaning of this representation, she may come up with all sorts of interpretations. Other pictorial symbols that may fox the children include white shapes on the sea on opening 1, meant to represent the ripples on the water, the large snowflakes falling on opening 6 and the dark colour wash on opening 9, to show that this is a night time picture. While it is generally best in a small group to let the children comment on what they find interesting, you could ask the children what they think these little lines and squiggles mean.

ASSESSMENT

Questions, comments and story-based discussion will help you to judge the child's level of understanding. How is the child interpreting the story and pictures? What sense is she making of the different themes of the book - the change in the seasons, weather, the passage of time, Sophie and her daddy's concurrent lives in different places, family life, letter writing and any other themes, topics or knowledge areas that emerge from your conversation?

EARLY LEARNING GOALS

Communication, Language and Literacy:
Listen with enjoyment, and respond to stories.
Enjoy listening to and using spoken and written language, and readily turn to it in their play and learning.
Sustain attentive listening, responding to what they have heard by relevant comments, questions or actions.
Use language to imagine and recreate roles and experiences.
Retell narratives in the correct sequence, drawing on language patterns of stories.
Show an understanding of the elements of stories, such as main character, sequence of events, and openings ...
Personal, Social and Emotional Development:
Maintain attention, concentrate and sit quietly when appropriate.
Knowledge and Understanding of the World:
Find out about, and identify, some features of living things, objects and events they observe.
Look closely at similarities, differences, patterns and change.

ACTIVITY - *Writing letters*

ABOUT THE ACTIVITY

Dear Daddy offers the children a number of facts about letters:
◆ the clever use of words and pictures makes it clear that a letter is written and sent to somebody who is far away from the sender;
◆ Sophie's letter has the traditional wording at the beginning and end: Dear ... and love from ...;
◆ opening 1 shows the envelope addressed to daddy on his ship in Hong Kong;
◆ opening 2 shows Sophie posting her letter;
◆ opening 3 shows the postman collecting letters from the post box;
◆ the content of Sophie's letter is typical, focusing on everyday events in her life, giving news about her family, wondering how daddy is and stating how much the family miss him.

All these details make the book a useful starting point for writing letters with your group. Sophie's letter can be used as a model, prompting the children to come up with their own ideas for the structure and content of a letter.

GROUP

No more than four children.

WHAT YOU WILL NEED

Dear Daddy
Clip-board, paper and marker pen
A selection of writing paper and envelopes
Stamps

WHAT TO DO

Talk about Sophie's letter. Look at how she starts it (Dear Daddy) and how she ends it (Love from Sophie). Talk about the kinds of things she writes in her letter - what she has been doing, what her mummy and Timmy have been doing and how much they all miss Daddy.

◆ **Who shall we write to?** Help the children to think of somebody to write to. Try to choose somebody well known to the children, whom they can envisage. If you are able to work with one child at a time, you could choose a relative. Ensure that whoever you pick is willing to write back. This gives the children the fun of receiving a reply and helps them realise that writing letters is a two-way process. Ensure that the recipient knows where to address their reply.

◆ **What shall we put?** Use your clip-board and pen so that you can write down the children's words. Start off with

Dear .... then ask each child one by one to tell you what she wants to say in the letter. Prompt if necessary by linking to Sophie's letter: Sophie told her daddy all about the weather. Perhaps the child could start off by telling what the weather is like today. Keep referring to the recipient as much as possible, to help the children grasp that they are communicating to a particular person - 'Mrs Evans will want to know all about our new climbing frame'. It can be useful to start off with older, more verbal children. This will help the rest of the group grasp the idea of what to do.

Once your letter has been composed, it needs to be written out neatly. Show the children a range of different writing papers, cards and envelopes and encourage them to choose appropriate paper. Write out the letter, preferably while the children are around so that they can become aware of what you are doing. This helps them to discover the purpose and process of writing. If you have any writers in your group, encourage them to help with as much of the writing as they can manage. All children who are able to write their own names can sign the bottom of the letter.

◆ **Sending the letter:** Show the children how to seal the letter in the envelope. Explain about writing the address on the front of the envelope, what the address is and why we have to add it. Look at the address on Sophie's letter (opening 1) and talk about house names and numbers, road names, town names and so on. You could extend the activity by taking small groups into the street to look at names and numbers and also to the post office, to buy a stamp. Show the children how and where to stick the stamp on their envelope and where to post the letter.

Explain to the children that the letters in the post box will be taken out by the postman, sorted and delivered. Link with the pictures of Sophie posting her letter on opening 2 and the postman emptying the letter box on opening 3. When you receive the reply to the children's letter, show them how the envelope is opened and look at the stamp, the postmark and the address as well as reading the contents.

Make a range of writing papers, pens, pencils, envelopes, cards, postcards and old stamps available so that the children can explore 'writing' their own letters. Look out for opportunities to send more letters, such as a thank-you letter after a visit, a 'get well' letter to a child who is unwell or even a 'pen pal' letter to a group in another part of the country.

ASSESSMENT
How appropriate is the child's contribution to the content of the letter and the recipient? Look out for signs that older children have grasped the concept of the letter as a written communication to a particular person. How fluently does the child express herself? Take into account age and whether English is the child's first language.

Once you have gone through the process of writing, addressing and sending your letter, look out for indications that children have remembered and understood the process. How do they use the post box and writing materials in your setting? Encourage them to use emergent writing to write their own letters. This will tell you how much they understand the process of writing and sending letters.

EARLY LEARNING GOALS
Communication, Language and Literacy:
Use their phonic knowledge to write simple regular words and make phonetically plausible attempts at more complex words.
Attempt writing for different purposes.
Write their own names and other things.
Enjoy listening to and using spoken and written language, and readily turn to it in their play and learning.
Sustain attentive listening, responding to what they have heard by relevant comments, questions or actions.
Use language to imagine and recreate roles and experiences.
Personal, Social and Emotional Development:
Be sensitive to the needs, views and feelings of others.
Consider the consequences of their words and actions for themselves and others.

A C T I V I T Y - *Exploring vehicles*

ABOUT THE ACTIVITY
The road that runs in front of Sophie's house has a constant flow of vehicles, with a different type appearing in each picture: post van, dustbin lorry, pick-up truck with wrecked car, delivery van, bicycles, bus and a range of cars. Add Daddy's ship and you have a wide selection of vehicles going about their daily business, making the book a good starting point for exploring vehicles.

GROUP
Up to six for talking about the vehicles in *Dear Daddy*; up to four at a time for drawing and painting vehicles and setting

up the display; as small a group as possible for 'Up, down, fast, slow'.

WHAT YOU WILL NEED
Dear Daddy
Pictures and photographs of different vehicles
Paints, pencils and paper
Clip-board, paper and marker pen
Toy vehicles
Different surfaces, such as sand, a tray of marbles, felt
Toy ramps

Dear Daddy

WHAT TO DO

Look at the different vehicles in *Dear Daddy* and show the children any other pictures of vehicles that you can gather - fire engine, ambulance, plane, motorbike, train. Discuss the vehicles with the children, looking at aspects such as size and colour, what they are used for, where and how they travel (air, water, road, tracks.) Pitch the level of your discussion so that it is appropriate for the age group. Very little ones can just focus on the vehicle itself - size, colour, the noise it might make and so on. Older ones can start thinking in more depth about the purpose of the vehicle (family transport, rescue, transport over long distances) and the element of travel (air, water, road, track).

MAKE A DISPLAY

Set up a 'vehicles' display. Paint and draw pictures of the different vehicles you have looked at and display these along with any other pictures and photographs you have been able to gather. Try to include pictures of tracks/road/sea and so on to go with the train/boat/car. Older children can help you plan written work to add to the display, giving information about the vehicles. Sit down with the clip-board and marker pen and make a note of their ideas to write up and add to the display.

Send a note home with the children asking for toy vehicles to be brought in. Decide how you are going to categorise vehicles. For example, vehicles that help us (fire engines, ambulances, dustbin lorries, post vans); vehicles for transport (cars, planes, trains, buses); emergency vehicles (police cars, ambulances, fire engines, helicopters). Involve the children as much as possible in mounting their pictures and arranging and setting out the display.

◆ UP, DOWN, FAST, SLOW

Toy vehicles give the child lots of opportunities to experience a number of scientific concepts and learn the different words that describe them. For example: up/down; push/pull; stop/go; fast/slow; speed up/slow down.

Let the children play freely with the vehicles in small groups and sit down with them from time to time to focus their attention on some of these concepts. Find out how much language they already know by asking them if they can make the car go fast, go slowly, stop and so on. Can they tell the difference between pushing and pulling their vehicle and are they able to identify these two different ways of creating force?

Provide them with different surfaces to play on and set challenges: Which does the car run best on - sand or the wooden floor? Felt or the table top? A tray with marbles or the same tray without marbles? Provide ramps and hills so that they can discover the difference between pushing the car uphill and letting it roll downhill.

If at all possible, let the children play with the vehicles on the floor. This makes it much easier for them to get down at eye level with the car and to feel more involved in their play.

Assessment

Use questions and comments to help you assess the child's level of understanding. How much does she draw on her previous experience and knowledge of vehicles? How enthusiastically does she bring in things from home and contribute to the display? Is she able to use criteria for sorting vehicles into their different categories?
How widely does the child explore the vehicles when left to play with them freely? Is she able to observe and talk about what happens when you set her challenges such as pushing the car up a toy ramp? Are older children able to predict what will happen and use appropriate language to describe their observations?

EARLY LEARNING GOALS

Knowledge and Understanding of the World:
Find out about, and identify, some features of living things, objects and events they observe.
Look closely at similarities, differences, patterns and change.
Ask questions about why things happen and how things work.
Communication, Language and Literacy:
Interact with others, negotiating plans and activities and taking turns in conversations.
Enjoy listening to and using spoken and written language, and readily turn to it in their play and learning.
Sustain attentive listening, responding to what they have heard by relevant comments, questions or actions.
Extend their vocabulary.
Mathematical Development:
Use everyday words to describe position.

A C T I V I T Y - *Weather charts*

ABOUT THE ACTIVITY

In the story, Sophie's daddy is away for a year and the pictures trace the four seasons, clearly showing the different types of weather. This makes the book a useful starting point for looking at the seasons and seasonal weather.

A weather chart is a good way of focusing attention on the weather and it can be used to record the weather from one day to the next. Making your own weather chart helps the children to feel more involved in the activity. Older ones can also be encouraged to think about how to symbolise each weather type in pictures. This ties in with the pictures in *Dear Daddy*, which use clear pictorial symbols to represent different weathers (lines for rain, curly tails on the leaves for wind, big white circles for snowflakes).

GROUP

For making the drawings, no more than four at a time; for using the chart, any reasonable number.

WHAT YOU WILL NEED

Dear Daddy
A large sheet of stiff card or hardboard
A laminator, sticky-backed plastic or felt
Glue
String
Paper, strong coloured card, pencils and pens in bright colours (wax, felt tips)
Blu-tack or Velcro

WHAT TO DO

Look at the pictures in *Dear Daddy* and talk about the different weather. Link to the children's own experiences as much as possible. If you are doing this activity in summer, you may choose to leave out the winter snow pictures.

Explain to the children that you are going to make a weather chart and that you need little pictures of all the different weathers. Make a list with the children of all the different weathers you can think of - sunny, rainy, windy. Depending on your age group, the season and the weather you have recently experienced, you could also add misty, snowy, thunder and lightning, cloudy, heavy rain, light showers, hail, rainbows.

Making the weather pictures: discuss with the children how to draw little pictures of each weather you want to show on your chart. Use *Dear Daddy* as a prompt by looking at how Philippe Dupasquier has depicted rain, wind and so on. Give the children small squares of paper to work on. Younger children may need to draw on larger sheets which can be cut out afterwards. Use bright colours for details such as suns and rainbows. Use different coloured paper to set off the different weathers - a pale blue background for your rainbow, or grey for your snowflakes.

Making the chart: the next stage is to make the chart itself. There are various possibilities, depending on what materials you have available and how you wish to attach the little weather pictures:

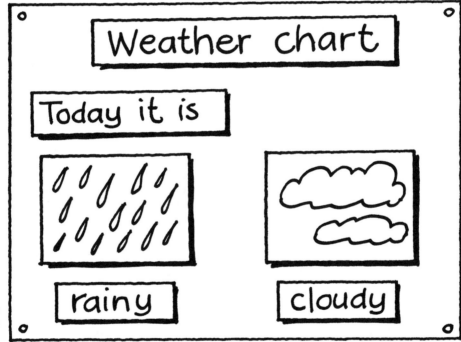

◆ **Laminated chart:** write your heading onto a sheet of thin card, such as 'Weather chart' and 'Today it is ...'. Laminate the sheet and attach a loop of string to the back so that you can hang it on the wall. The children's small pictures can also be laminated and then stuck onto the chart with Blu-tack.

◆ **Felt chart:** cover a piece of hardboard or heavy duty card with felt and glue your heading onto the felt. Mount the children's little weather pictures on stiff card and glue Velcro hooks to the back of each card. The pictures can then be pressed onto the felt surface. If you use hardboard, make sure your string loop is firmly attached. Alternatively, prop it up on a book stand.

◆ **Plastic-covered chart:** cover a sheet of card with sticky-backed plastic (available from DIY or stationery shops). If you use clear plastic, write your headings onto the card before covering it. If you use a coloured and patterned plastic, glue your headings onto the plastic. The children's pictures can then be mounted and fixed with Blu-tack onto the surface.

Dear Daddy

Once you have finished your chart, show the children how to use it. Talk about the weather and select the appropriate pictures. Show the children where to put the pictures on the chart. You can either use just one representation at a time, making sure that every child's picture is put up at some point or, if you have a big chart, you can put up all the sunny pictures/rainy pictures or whatever represents the day's weather.

Make some word labels to add - 'sunny', 'rainy', 'windy' and so on. Help older children who are starting to read to choose the correct label to go with the picture.

If you want to do a survey of the week's weather, make five little charts with the name of each weekday on the top. You can then look back over the week with the children to see how the weather has changed. Doing this will also help the children learn the days of the week.

ASSESSMENT

To what extent does the child draw on her own experiences of different weathers to contribute to the discussion? Are older children able to recognise the little pictures as representing different weathers? Are they able to suggest their own ways of drawing the weather?

How accurately are the children able to observe and identify the weather and choose the appropriate picture to put up on the chart?

EARLY LEARNING GOALS

Knowledge and Understanding of the World:
Observe, find out about and identify features in the place they live and the natural world.
Find out about, and identify, some features of living things, objects and events they observe.
Ask questions about why things happen and how things work.
Look closely at similarities, differences, patterns and change.

Communication, Language and Literacy:
Sustain attentive listening, responding to what they have heard by relevant comments, questions or actions.
Extend their vocabulary.

Creative Development:
Respond in a variety of ways to what they see, hear, smell, touch and feel.
Explore colour, texture, shape, form and space in two or three dimensions.

Physical Development:
Handle tools, objects, construction and malleable materials safely and with increasing control.

FIVE-MINUTE ACTIVITIES

WEATHER MOVEMENTS

Talk about what we do and how we feel when it is hot, cold, rainy and windy. Practise some movements and mimes - for example, wiping foreheads and sighing when it is sweltering; shivering, wrapping arms around you and stamping when it is very cold; being blown about when it is windy. Add some appropriate background music to help set the scene.

MATCHING VEHICLES AND SETTINGS

Gather a range of pictures to match with the toy vehicles in your setting - a sky to go with the plane or helicopter; a burning building to go with the fire engine; a road to go with the car; a hospital to go with the ambulance; a farm scene to go with the tractor; a street with a post box to go with the post van; railway tracks to go with the train; sea or river to go with the boat. If you have difficulty finding pictures, take photographs. You can also do your own drawings or get someone to do them for you. Mount the pictures and then show the children how to match the pictures with the vehicles. If your pictures are large and you can laminate them, they could be used as play mats to go with the vehicles.

POST BOX

Make a post box for your setting. Cover a box with red paper and cut out a slit. Provide a peaked cap and brown bag or satchel for children to role play being post people (like the postman on opening 3 of *Dear Daddy*.) Encourage the children to post letters and pictures to each other. Emphasise the importance of writing the name of the recipient on each letter - ensure that the children ask an adult for help with this. Organise one or two children to empty and sort the letters ready for delivery at the end of each session (see *Who's Who in Our Street?*, 'Making a roster' page 76).

About Who's Who in Our Street?

Like Philippe Dupasquier's *Dear Daddy*, *Who's Who in Our Street?* is a complex book with lots of details to look at and talk about.

The words and pictures tell the story of a week in the lives of three families who all live in the same street. Mums, dads, older brothers and sisters help each other out; younger ones play together and everyone has fun with the pets. In many ways, this delightful book is a soap opera for the pre-school age group.

As you work your way through the pages, it becomes easier to recognise and name each character. Older children will enjoy the challenge of trying to identify different people and work out who belongs to which family - particularly if you set about answering the many questions in the text: Who is looking after whom? Who ate Jock's supper? (tip: the members of each family share the same initial letter - Bill, Biddy, Bea; Jenny, Josh, Jake and so on.)

Although Jan Ormerod's style is quite different to Shirley Hughes', she has a similar knack when it comes to capturing the spirit of young children in her drawings. The different characters seem to leap off the page so that it is easy for the child to become engrossed in the everyday detail of their lives. Like *Dear Daddy*, you will get the most out of this book if you can share it with a small group and allow the children as long as they need to study the pictures and talk about the story.

A C T I V I T Y - *A weekly diary*

ABOUT THE ACTIVITY

Pre-school children are not usually ready to think about the measurement of time in terms of minutes and hours, but they can be introduced to a day and a week. These are blocks of time that can be linked with their own experiences.

Focusing on the order of events in a typical day makes a good starting point. This helps the child develop a sense of what a day consists of as well as the idea of time passing. Within the day, you can highlight smaller blocks of time, such as being at pre-school in the morning.

Other than the day, the most relevant block of time in the child's life is the week. Making a diary is a useful way of introducing the child to the concept of the week because you can draw on the child's daily experiences. The activity can be linked with *Who's Who in Our Street?* because the book is structured around the seven days of the week.

GROUP

Up to four children for looking at the events of a day; any reasonable number for listing the events of the week; up to four children for making drawings and paintings of weekly events.

WHAT YOU WILL NEED

Who's Who in Our Street?
Clip-board, paper and marker pen
Drawings or pictures of typical events that take place during a single day (optional)
Seven sheets of mounting paper, a minimum of two different colours
Materials for drawing and painting
Glue and scissors.

WHAT TO DO

◆ **A day:** with your children, make a list of the regular and routine things that happen on a single day - getting out of bed, having breakfast, cleaning teeth, coming to playgroup. You can then work through the order of events during your pre-school morning or day - circle time, play, snack, going into the garden. Help the children to focus on the sequence of events within a day by making little drawings for them to put in order. For example, cleaning teeth, arriving at playgroup, circle time, eating lunch, night-time bath, going to bed.

◆ **A week:** the next stage is to survey the regular and routine things that take place on each day of the week. You will probably need to do this in a separate session. Start off by looking at *Who's Who in Our Street?* with your group, highlighting the different days of the week and one or two events that take place.

Go on to compile a list of the special things that happen on each day. If you have children who do not attend every day of the week, this makes a good starting point: Jamie, Lara, Kumar, Charlotte, Dean, Aisha, Mrs Andrews and Miss Annie come to pre-school on Monday. Do this for each day of the week, to give the children the chance to associate the separate days with a personal experience. Add to your list the significant events in the pre-school week: cleaning out the hamster on Mondays, somebody special coming to do craft on Tuesdays, a walk to the park on Wednesday. Every group will have its own, unique weekly programme. Try to get across the idea that these events occur again and again as a cycle.

You will also need to look at the weekend if you are going to survey the whole week. For children who only attend on two or three mornings a week, highlight elements such as mummy or daddy not going to work, older brothers and sisters not going to school, weekend activities such as family trips, visiting church, a special Saturday or Sunday meal. In *Who's Who in Our Street?*, the families do typical weekend things such as going to the park, decorating and having Sunday lunch with Granny. This is a good opportunity to talk about different home lives, particularly if you have a mixed-race group of children.

MAKE A DISPLAY

Choose seven large sheets of coloured paper so that each of the seven days is a different colour from those next to it. Write the name of each day at the top of the sheet. Write out the special things that happen on each day to add to the sheets. Ask the children to draw or paint pictures of the activities to stick alongside the writing. You could also ask the children to bring in photographs of themselves. These can be fixed with blu-tack on to the appropriate days as a record of who is at pre-school on which day. Ask any children who can write their names to do so and stick these beside their photographs.

Put up the sheets of paper on the wall in the correct order. Refer to them as often as possible to reinforce the days that make up the week. If you have a large expanse of wall, arrange them in a circular shape to represent the week as a cycle that continually repeats itself.

Leave a space on each sheet and encourage older children to think of and add new events as the term progresses.

ASSESSMENT

What contribution does each child make to your discussion about the events of the day and the events of the week? Is the child able to put the day's events in order?

Once you have put up your display, do you need to prompt older ones to suggest daily events to add or do they come up with ideas independently? As you look at and go through the display and other weekday activities, look out for signs that the older child is grasping the concept of 'day' and 'week'.

EARLY LEARNING GOALS

Knowledge and Understanding of the World:
Find out about, and identify, some features of living things, objects and events they observe.
Look closely at similarities, differences, patterns and change.
Communication, Language and Literacy:
Sustain attentive listening, responding to what they have heard by relevant comments, questions or actions.
Extend their vocabulary ...
Creative Development:
Explore colour, texture, shape, form and space in two or three dimensions.
Physical Development:
Handle tools, objects, construction and malleable materials safely and with increasing control.
Mathematical Development:
In practical activities and discussion begin to use the vocabulary involved in adding and subtracting.

ACTIVITY - *Making a roster*

ABOUT THE ACTIVITY

The story of *Who's Who in Our Street?* revolves around everybody helping each other. The washing-up roster on opening 8 shows how one family co-operates and it can be used as the starting point for making your own roster with older children. This simple activity introduces the idea of everybody taking it in turns to do chores, as well as ensuring that the chores are distributed fairly. It also reinforces the names and the sequence of the days of the week.

GROUP

Up to five children at a time.

WHAT YOU WILL NEED

Who's Who in Our Street?
Charts, made from large sheets of paper, preferably laminated or covered in clear plastic (see illustration)
Strips of card for writing labels
Strips of card for writing names or coloured stars / stickers
Blu-tack
Clip-board, paper and marker pen

WHAT TO DO

Begin by talking about helping out at home. What jobs do

the children do to help mum and dad? Do they share tasks with brothers and sisters? Link with some of the ways in which characters in the story help out: Jake grating the cheese on opening 7; Biddy and Boo Boo looking after Mickey when he is sick on opening 4. Show the children the roster on opening 8 and talk about how it works.

Move on to the topic of helping out at pre-school and make a list of jobs that have to be done, encouraging the children

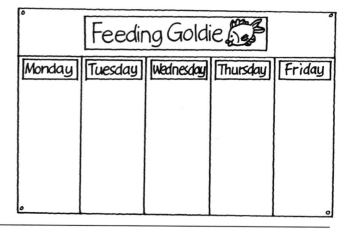

to contribute as much as possible. Some examples might be: feeding pets; handing out cups at snack time; clearing away plates after lunch; sorting the pencils into their colour pots; fetching the drawings and paintings to be handed out at home time; watering the plants.

If your children are not already doing little tasks to help in the smooth running of the group, this activity makes a good starting point.

Show your children the roster chart you have made. Point out the days of the week written across the top and the space for names or stickers. Choose a task, such as handing out cups, and write the name of the task on a strip of card so that it can be attached to the top of the chart. You could also add a little drawing of the task. You then need to decide on how to identify the children. They could write their names on strips to be attached to the appropriate day, or they could each have a different coloured star (as in *Who's Who in Our Street?*) or a different sticker - or both name and sticker. If you go for just the sticker, keep a list in case the children forget which is theirs.

Choose a day for each child to carry out the task. If your children do not attend every day, remember to make sure the child is with you on the morning they are allotted. Ask the children to come and stick their names or stickers in the appropriate place. Pin the chart to the wall and check it each morning so that everybody knows whose turn it is. Make as many charts as you wish to cover the various shared tasks in your setting. If you can laminate or cover them in clear plastic, they can be used time after time for different

activities - simply stick on a label with the name and picture of the task. If a task needs to be carried out by more than one child at a time, make the chart bigger so that there is room for two names or stickers on each day. Encourage the children to look out for tasks that need doing and could be delegated amongst all the children in the group.

ASSESSMENT
Is the child able to draw on her own experiences of being helpful at home to contribute to the discussion? Is she able to identify the kinds of tasks that are helpful at pre-school? How fluently and confidently does she express herself during the discussion?

Once the chart has been made, is the older child able to use it each day to work out whose turn it is to carry out a task? Look out for signs that she is learning the days of the week.

EARLY LEARNING GOALS
Personal, Social and Emotional Development:
Work as part of a group or class, taking turns and sharing fairly, understanding that there needs to be agreed values and codes of behaviour for groups of people, including adults and children, to work together harmoniously.
Communication, Language and Literacy:
Interact with others, negotiating plans and activities and taking turns in conversation.
Extend their vocabulary.
Knowledge and Understanding of the World:
Find out about, and identify, some features of living things, objects and events they observe.

ACTIVITY - *Rooms in a house*

ABOUT THE ACTIVITY
The events in *Who's Who in Our Street?* take place against a typical domestic background, showing some realistic snapshots of various rooms and gardens. The pictures in the book can be used as a starting point for looking at the different rooms in a house and thinking about their purpose.

GROUP
Up to four children.

WHAT YOU WILL NEED
Who's Who in Our Street?
House shapes cut out of sugar paper and divided into four rooms (see illustration)
Pictures of furniture cut out from catalogues
Glue
Paint, printing sponges, potatoes, wood blocks, wallpaper pieces, coloured card or paper for making trees, street lamps and road (optional)

WHAT TO DO
Look at pictures of different rooms in *Who's Who in Our Street?* For example, opening 3 shows a kitchen table at breakfast time and a garden with rabbits and guinea pigs; opening 5 shows a scene from a bedroom and opening 6 shows part of a sitting room.

Talk about the rooms in a house, such as the bedroom, the sitting room, the kitchen, the bathroom. Some children may not have realised that each room in their house has a different name and a different purpose. Help the child to identify the different rooms by talking about furniture and other household items, and the key activities that take place in each room - sleeping and playing in the bedroom, preparing food in the kitchen, washing in the bathroom and so on. Draw on the children's own experiences as much as possible. You could also link this part of your discussion with the story, such as Biddie cooking in the kitchen in opening six.

Give the children a house shape cut out from sugar paper and divided into four sections. Older children can be encouraged to draw and cut out their own shapes. Explain to the children that the sections represent a bedroom, a sitting room, a kitchen and a bathroom - the four most distinctive rooms in a house.

Give the children a collection of pictures cut out from a catalogue. Include several items for each room, such as:

- **bedroom** - bed, bedside lamp, duvet, chest of drawers, pillow
- **sitting room** - sofa, tv, standard lamp, chair, cushion, coffee table
- **bathroom** - toilet, basin, towel, bath, bathroom cabinet, bath mat
- **kitchen** - cooker, fridge, microwave, plates, washing machine

Help the children to decide which item should go in which room, reminding them of the name and purpose of each room if necessary. Once a child has decided where a picture should go, she can stick it in the appropriate room. If you have children who are ready to cut out their own furniture pictures, give them single sheets torn out of the catalogues. Older children can also draw and cut out their own pictures and write labels for the different items of furniture. Some items can go in more than one room - a lamp or a cushion could go in the bedroom or the sitting room, for example. Go with the child's decision but take the opportunity to talk about how the item would fit into either room.

MAKE A DISPLAY
Stick the houses on the wall in a row to make a street. Make the display more decorative by using some of the following ideas:

- Add some cut-out and painted trees, street lamps and a strip of black paper to make a road.
- Print red tiles onto the roofs with a potato cut into a rectangle or the edge of a block of wood (before the children stick on their furniture).
- Sponge print the rooms in different colours or cut out sheets of wallpaper to glue onto each room (before the children stick on their furniture).
- Fold the sugar paper in two and cut out the house shape as if it were a greetings card. Cut windows and a door in the front (see illustration). Paint or sponge print the front of the card in suitable colours. The inside can then be divided

into rooms for the furniture. Secure the front with a blob of Blu-tack when putting it on the wall.

ASSESSMENT
Is the child able to draw on her knowledge and experience of her own home to contribute to the discussion about different rooms? How fluently and confidently is she able to express herself?

When sorting pictures of household items into different rooms, how much help does the child need in deciding which item of furniture should go in which room? Is she starting to realise that each room has its own name and purpose?

Look out for how the child handles scissors and glue (see Assessment, 'Animal flaps' page 30).

EARLY LEARNING GOALS
Knowledge and Understanding of the World:
Find out about their environment, and talk about those features they like and dislike.
Find out about past and present events in their own lives, and in those of their families and other people they know.
Look closely at similarities, differences, patterns and change.
Communication, Language and Literacy:
Interact with others, negotiating plans and activities and taking turns in conversation.
Extend their vocabulary.
Creative Development:
Explore colour, texture, shape, form and space in two or three dimensions.
Physical Development:
Handle tools, objects, construction and malleable materials safely and with increasing control.

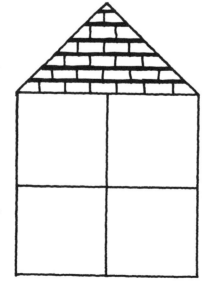

A C T I V I T Y - *All kinds of houses*

ABOUT THE ACTIVITY

The previous activity looked at the interior of a typical house, using the setting of *Who's Who in Our Street?* as the starting point. This activity moves on to look at different types of houses and buildings, beginning with what is most familiar to the child - her own home. Just as the 'Rooms in a house' activity encourages the child to organise and classify her home environment, these activities help her to make sense of her wider environment through naming and grouping different types of buildings and thinking about their purpose.

GROUP

Any reasonable number for introducing and talking about pictures of buildings; just one or two at a time for 'The child's own house'; as small a child/adult ratio as possible for the walk; up to four children at a time for printing and collage pictures of buildings.

WHAT YOU WILL NEED

Who's Who in Our Street?
The child's own house activity: photographs of each child's home; paper for making notes and writing out child's words about her house; coloured card or sugar paper and glue for mounting.
Different types of buildings - an introduction: pictures of different houses and buildings from books and magazines, postcards and photographs.
Different types of buildings - a walk: camera (optional); sugar paper, paint, printing materials and collage materials (see below).

WHAT TO DO

The child's own house: send a note home asking for the child to bring in a photograph of her house/ bungalow/flat. Working with just one or two children at a time, talk about the pictures with the child and make notes of what she says about her home, prompting her with questions if necessary. Encourage her to notice and talk about the features of the building. This can also be a good opportunity to introduce or reinforce the names of different parts of a house - the roof, windows, walls, front door and so on.

Different types of buildings - an introduction: once you have looked at the children's own houses, you can move on to different types of buildings. Gather a collection of pictures. Some possibilities include: flats, bungalows, offices, tower blocks, churches and other places of worship, farm houses, leisure centres, garages. Don't try to cover everything. At this stage, aim to reflect the child's environment. For example, tower blocks and a temple for the inner-city child, stone built cottages and a village hall for the rural child. See if the children can name the different buildings and talk about their purposes.

Use books, magazines, postcards and photographs as sources for your pictures. Estate agents may be willing to let you have old photographs of different properties. Postcards tend to feature more unusual, picturesque or important buildings.

Different types of buildings - a walk: once you have looked at and talked about pictures of different types of buildings, take the children for a walk to look at some buildings. Choose your route carefully. Apart from safety, you need to pick an area that has more than one type of building. Enlist as many parents and helpers as possible. The smaller your adult/child ratio on a trip like this, the more the children will gain through asking questions and receiving pointers as to what to look out for.

Make a preliminary trip and list the particular buildings you want to look at. Do they have any special and interesting features? What are their different purposes? Do the children and their families already use them? (This might apply to places of worship, shops, leisure centres.) If possible, take photographs or even a video to remind the children of the different buildings they saw. Give each helper a list of the things you would like them to point out to the children.

During the walk, introduce appropriate vocabulary such as *pavement, road, zebra crossing, shop, flats, offices, town, village, park.* Older children can be shown and told the names of different building materials - stone, brick, wood, tiles, thatch, glass.

MAKE A DISPLAY

The child's own house: mount the photograph of the child's house on a piece of coloured paper. Write out the child's comments about her house to stick beside the photograph (in the rare event of a child making a negative comment about her home, it may be wise not to include this in the writing). Any children who are ready can copy out some statements or even write a few of their own words, depending on age group/level of writing development.

Different types of buildings - an introduction: mount the different pictures you have gathered. Ask the children to help you sort them into groups and display them on the wall with a label to name each group. If you are able to laminate the pictures, they can be used year after year and you can keep on adding to your collection.

Different types of buildings - a walk: choose certain buildings from your walk to use for an art project. Go for contrasting buildings with distinctive features. For example, a church, a tower block, a bungalow, a couple of different houses. If you were able to take photographs, study these with the children and talk about the colours, shapes, sizes and features of the buildings you are going to focus on. Plan different art techniques for decorating the buildings: sponge print to create a rough stony texture; stick on rectangles of coloured paper to represent tiles and bricks; make windows out of silver foil; make stained glass windows out of coloured tissue or crepe paper; stick on buttons for door handles; use straw for thatched roofs; spread glue onto the paper and sprinkle on sand for paths; use textured white wallpaper to create a stuccoed effect. Provide a variety of materials and encourage the children to choose what they think is appropriate to create different effects.

You can either give a small group a large cut-out building shape to decorate together or each child can have their own smaller shape to decorate. The buildings can then be put up on the wall in a row to represent a street. Add street lamps, trees and a strip of grey paper to make a pavement.

ASSESSMENT

The child's own house: how fluently can the child talk about her home? Is she able to lead the conversation or does she rely on your prompting? Does she know the names of different parts of the house?

Different types of buildings - a walk: make a note of how closely the child can follow instructions during the walk. How does she conduct herself in the environment beyond the setting? Does she ask questions and make comments? What contribution does she make to a follow up discussion?

Make a display: how does the child handle collage and printing techniques (See Assessment for 'Animal flaps', page 30 and 'Printing handkerchiefs', page 27)? Is the older child

able to choose appropriate techniques to decorate the different buildings?

EARLY LEARNING GOALS

Knowledge and Understanding of the World:
Find out about, and identify, some features of living things, objects and events they observe.
Look closely at similarities, differences, patterns and change.

Communication, Language and Literacy:
Enjoy listening to and using spoken and written language, and readily turn to it in their play and learning.
Sustain attentive listening, responding to what they have heard by relevant comments, questions or actions.
Extend their vocabulary.

Creative Development:
Explore colour, texture, shape, form and space in two or three dimensions.
Express and communicate their ideas, thoughts and feelings by using a widening range of materials, suitable tools ... designing and making.

Physical Development:
Handle tools, objects, construction and malleable materials safely and with increasing control.

FIVE-MINUTE ACTIVITIES

PARTS OF A BUILDING

Make a large simple drawing of a house or cut one out of a magazine. Mount the picture on card and cut it into pieces so that the different parts are separate - roof, windows, door, walls, chimney. With a small group, put the pieces together, naming the separate parts as you go along. Secure each piece onto a board with Blu-tack if necessary.

WHO'S HERE TODAY?

At the start of each day, name the day and go through those children who are at school on that morning. Adapt the 'Today's Monday' song to list the children:

Today's Monday, today's Monday
Gemma's at school today
Rachel's at school today
Mrs Andrew's at school today
Miss Annie's at school today ......
We're all happy
To be at school today.

Work your way around the circle and

encourage the children to join in with the song. If necessary, change school to pre-school, playgroup or whatever name is appropriate for your setting.

BEING HELPFUL

Who's Who in Our Street? is bursting with information about how the lives of friends, neighbours and families interweave and touch each other. Much of this is based on characters helping each other out, ranging from a dad babysitting while the mums take a break in the garden to teenagers walking the younger ones to school. The book can be used as the starting point for an exploration of 'being helpful'. Substitute *Who's Who in Our Street?* for *Farmer Duck* (see page 81) and follow a similar procedure.

SORTING HOUSEHOLD ITEMS

Cut out pictures of household items from a catalogue and mount onto card. If possible, laminate or cover with plastic. Choose distinctive items that can be clearly identified as belonging to a bedroom, a kitchen, a bathroom and a sitting room. Help the children to sort the cards into groups, according to which room they belong in. If you have a dolls' house, the cards could be sorted by placing them into the appropriate rooms. The children can also match the cards with corresponding dolls' house furniture.

About Farmer Duck

Farmer Duck **brings together two of the most famous names in the picture book world: the writer Martin Waddell and the illustrator Helen Oxenbury.**

The repetitive text is simple but beautifully written. It tells the story of a lazy farmer who leaves the poor duck to do all the work. Everything ends happily when the rest of the animals hatch a plan to rescue the duck and get their own back on the farmer. Unusually for a children's book, the animals communicate only in moos, baas, quacks and clucks, leaving the narrator and the pictures to relate the story. When they return from sorting out the farmer, the animals tell the duck what has happened with a moo! a baa! and a cluck! - 'which told the duck the whole story'. This clever device encourages the children to remember and fill in what has happened for themselves - an important skill when it comes to making sense of stories.

The pictures are as delightful as the stories. The pages are cream coloured and you can see the pencil strokes and the delicate watercolours set against stippled paper. The animals manage to show facial expressions and human movement without losing their essential animal appearance.

The two main themes of the book link with Personal, Social and Emotional Development (helping each other and sharing tasks) and Knowledge and Understanding of the World (farms and farmyard animals).

A C T I V I T Y - *Farmyard patchwork*

ABOUT THE ACTIVITY
This activity uses a range of painting, printing and collage techniques to make farmyard animals and fields. The pictures can then be arranged in a patchwork pattern. Creating pictures of the different animals encourages the children to think about and explore their features. The range of techniques enables you to tailor the different parts of the activity to suit different age and ability levels.

GROUP
Up to four children at a time.

WHAT YOU WILL NEED
Farmer Duck and pictures of animals not featured in the story
Farm animal templates (optional)
Card in various colours, including black
Cotton wool
Sponge pieces, carrots and thick paint brushes
Broken eggshells
Feathers
Pink, white, brown, green and yellow paint
Gift wrap ribbon
Squares of sugar paper in shades of brown, green and blue
Sand
Tissue paper in shades of blue and white
Silver paper
String and wood blocks
Pressed flowers and grasses
Scissors
Glue

WHAT TO DO
Decide on the animals you want to make and look carefully at pictures of each animal with the children. Talk about colour, shape, size and features. Try the following ideas:

◆ **Sheep:** stick pieces of cotton wool onto ready-cut shapes.

Make faces and legs from black card. Use raw sheep's wool as a more authentic alternative to cotton wool.

◆ **Cows:** print black splodges onto cut-out shapes with a small piece of sponge, a section of carrot or the end of a thick paint brush.

◆ **Hens:** stick pieces of eggshell onto cut-out hen shapes. If you have access to feathers, add these to the hens' tails.

◆ **Ducks:** sponge print brilliant white paint onto cut-out duck shapes and paint on a bright yellow beak.

◆ **Pigs:** paint cut-out pig shapes pink. Curl thin strips of gift wrap ribbon with the back of a knife to make tails.

Once you have made the animals, they will need some fields. Cut squares of paper, all the same size. If possible, use a range of greens and browns. Decorate the squares using some of the following ideas:

◆ **Grass:** stick on thin strips of green paper to make grass. Make a string block by gluing lengths of string onto a chunk of wood and print with green paint to represent grass.

◆ **Ploughed fields:** print rows of splodges with a piece of sponge. Rule guidelines for the children to print along. Use brown paint on brown paper.

◆ **Sand:** spread glue onto a square of sandy yellow paper and sprinkle on sand or small gravel, like glitter.

◆ **Flowers:** take the children into the garden or for a nature walk. Gather flowers, grasses and leaves and press them for one to two weeks inside heavy books. Once dry, they can be stuck onto one of the green squares.

Farmer Duck

◆ **Wheat field:** print with a string block or make single strokes of yellow paint with a thick paint brush to represent the stalks of wheat.

◆ **Pond:** cut out a pond shape from blue paper and stick it to one of the squares. Stick pieces of blue and white tissue paper and pieces of silver foil onto the pond to make the water.

Once you have finished your backgrounds, decide with the children where the different animals should go - the ducks on the pond, the pigs in the ploughed field, the cows amongst the wheat, the sheep in the grassy field, the hens amongst the flowers. Fix the animals to their backgrounds with Blu-tack and then mount them on the wall side by side like tiles. The patchwork effect and the different shapes, colours and textures will look stunning when displayed in your setting. Encourage the children to think of a name for their patchwork farm.

ASSESSMENT
Observe how the child handles scissors, glue and printing techniques (see Assessment for 'Animal flaps' page 30 and 'Printing handkerchiefs' page 27).
Can the older child choose appropriate techniques and materials for the particular animal she is making?

EARLY LEARNING GOALS
Creative Development:
Explore colour, texture, shape, form and space in two or three dimensions.
Express and communicate their ideas, thoughts and feelings by using a widening range of materials, suitable tools ... designing and making.
Physical Development:
Handle tools, objects, construction and malleable materials safely and with increasing control.
Knowledge and Understanding of the World:
Find out about, and identify, some features of living things, objects and events they observe.
Build and construct with a wide range of objects, selecting appropriate resources, and adapting their work where necessary.
Select the tools and techniques they need to shape, assemble and join materials they are using.

ACTIVITY - *Farmyard lotto*

ABOUT THE ACTIVITY
Lotto games are simple to make and offer the children a number of useful learning experiences, including turn taking, matching skills and conversation about the theme of the game. If older children can help to make the game, it will add to their involvement in the activity as a whole. This lotto game uses the theme of farm animals and the noises they make.

GROUP
Up to three children.

WHAT YOU WILL NEED
Farmer Duck
A tape recorder and tape
Animal templates or pictures
Four A4 sheets of card
Twelve small squares of card
Ruler
Black marker pen
Scissors
Colouring pencils
Glue

WHAT TO DO
Making the game: start off by preparing a tape of animal noises:
◆ a duck quacking
◆ a cow mooing
◆ a donkey braying
◆ a horse neighing
◆ a hen clucking
◆ a cat mewing
◆ a dog barking
◆ a sheep baaing
◆ a pig oinking

Record the noises one after the other in random order, leaving a short gap in between each one. Once you have finished all nine, repeat the process but use a different order. (It is a good idea to make some indication on the tape that you have finished one set before you begin a new set.) If farmyard impressions are not your forte, find someone who can do them for you.

Divide three sheets of card into four equal squares, using a thick black marker pen. If you are using A4 card, you will need to trim one end. You will need enough animals to stick one on each square of the large cards plus a matching separate card (see illustration). You can organise the animals in any way you wish but you do need to ensure that each of the three cards has a different combination. Try the following:
◆ **Card 1** - horse, donkey, sheep, hen
◆ **Card 2** - duck, pig, hen, dog
◆ **Card 3** - cow, cat, dog, sheep

If you use this order, you will need pictures of two horses, two donkeys, two ducks, two pigs, two cows, two cats, four sheep, four hens and four dogs.

Ask the children to colour in the drawings. Cut them out and stick one of each pair onto a large card and one onto a small card. Involve the children as much as possible. Older children with good drawing skills could also draw some of the animals themselves - although you won't end up with pictures that are an exact match. Get round this by mounting the pairs of animals on matching colours so that the child can use colour as well as type to match each pair.

If you have access to a laminator or you can cover the cards with clear plastic, your game will last much longer.

Playing the game: start off by looking at the different animals in *Farmer Duck* and go through the noises they make. Talk about the other animals you will be using in the game - the pig, the donkey, the horse, the cat and the dog.

Give each child a large card and spread out the small cards in the centre of the table. Start the tape and listen to the first animal noise. Help the children to identify the noise and the animal that made it. If they wish, they can try making the noise themselves. Ask them to look on their large cards. If they have that animal, they can find the matching card and place it in the appropriate square of their large card. Continue until all nine noises have been played. The winner is the first one to complete their card.

ASSESSMENT

Is the child able to sit quietly and listen to the tape? Once the animal has been identified, is she able to find the appropriate picture and match it with the picture on her card? Can she name the animal?

EARLY LEARNING GOALS

Knowledge and Understanding of the World:
Find out about, and identify, some features of living things, objects and events they observe.

Look closely at similarities, differences, patterns and change.
Communication, Language and Literacy:
Enjoy listening to and using spoken and written language, and readily turn to it in their play and learning.
Sustain attentive listening, responding to what they have heard by relevant comments, questions or actions.
Extend their vocabulary.
Personal, Social and Emotional Development:
Work as part of a group or class, taking turns and sharing fairly, understanding that there needs to be agreed values and codes of behaviour for groups of people, including adults and children, to work together harmoniously.
Creative Development:
Respond in a variety of ways to what they see, hear, smell, touch and feel.

A C T I V I T Y - *Farm produce*

ABOUT THE ACTIVITY

Farmer Duck can be used as the starting point for exploring farm animals and helping the children link farming with some of the foods and other products that they come across on a daily basis. Sheep, hens, cows and wheat make the easiest farm animals and crops to explore with this age group because they all produce food and clothing that is familiar to the child.

GROUP

Any reasonable number for looking at different animals. No more than four at a time for follow-up activities.

WHAT YOU WILL NEED

Farmer Duck
Sheep - sheep's wool, knitting yarn and needles, knitted items, models of sheep
Cows - full cream milk, butter, jar with tight lid, models of cows
Hens - eggs, pictures of life-cycle of hen (see template on page 89), circle of coloured paper, glue, red felt pen
Wheat - ears of wheat, flour, bread, ingredients and utensils for making bread (see below)
Making a display - cotton wool, strips of card, glue, scissors, drawing materials

Farmer Duck

WHAT TO DO
Choose one or more of the following to explore with your children, depending on whether you want this to be a short or an extended topic.

◆ **Sheep:** look at the pictures of the sheep in the story. Talk about what they eat, where they live and their woolly coats. If possible, get some sheep's wool to show the children. If you live near sheep farming country, it is easy to gather bits of wool from barbed wire fences. Craft shops also sometimes sell raw wool.

Older children can be shown how the wool is washed in detergent, carded (brushed to get all the fibres in the same direction) and spun (twisted to make into yarn). Folk museums often employ traditional craftspeople who can do a demonstration for the children.

Show the children a ball of knitting wool, knitting needles and some knitted items. Do a survey of who in the group is wearing knitted clothes.

Gather a model sheep, a piece of raw wool, a ball of wool with knitting needles and a knitted item and help the children to put them in order.

◆ **Cows:** (Before beginning this activity check that no child has a dairy allergy.) Look at the pictures of the cow in the story. Use a model cow to show the children the udders that give milk. Show the children some milk and make the link between the cow and the milk. Talk about other milk-based products - butter, cheese, yoghurt, cream, custard, ice cream.

You can make your own butter by putting full cream milk in a jar with a tight lid and shaking vigorously until the butter separates from the buttermilk. Rinse the butter granules with very cold water and pat into shape. The process is quite lengthy. Although all the children can have a turn at shaking, try to ensure you have plenty of adult helpers around to keep things going.

Gather a model cow, a carton of milk and butter and ask the children to put them in order.

◆ **Hens:** look at the pictures of the hens in the story. Make the link between hens and eggs. (See Rosie's Walk 'Hens and eggs' activity (page 59) for some ideas on how to present the life-cycle of a hen to young children.)

◆ **Wheat:** (Before beginning this activity, check that no child has a wheat allergy.) Opening 19 shows all the animals harvesting wheat from the field. Look at the picture with the children and explain that wheat is grown on lots of farms. Show the children some ears of wheat. If you live near wheat fields, beg a few stalks from the farmer. Dried flower displays and corn dollies make another good source of wheat. Show the children the grains of wheat.

Explain to older children that the wheat is ground to make flour and show them some flour. Talk about the different foods flour is used for - bread, cakes, pastry, pancakes. Show the children a loaf of bread.

Gather an ear of wheat, flour and bread and ask the children to put them in order. Try a recipe with the children using flour. If you can co-ordinate making butter (see above) with baking bread, the children can taste their own butter on their own bread.

MAKE A DISPLAY
Sheep: ask the children to make little drawings of sheep, raw wool, a ball of wool and a knitted item. Stick them onto strips of paper in the correct order. Make the display look more decorative by making cotton-wool sheep (see 'Farmyard patchwork'), sticking on real raw wool, a ball of wool and knitted item to stiff card to pin up on the wall.

Cows: give each child in your group a circle of sugar paper. Ask them to draw a cow to cut out and stick at the top of the circle. Go through lots of magazines for pictures of dairy foods to cut out and stick on the circle beneath the cow.

Hens: see *Rosie's Walk* 'Hens and eggs' activity (page 59) for some display ideas.

Wheat: make little drawings of ears of wheat, flour and bread to stick onto strips of paper. Alternatively, you could pin up real wheat, sprinkle wholemeal flour onto glue (like glitter) and pin slices of bread to stiff card. The bread will need changing if you keep the display up for a while. Glue the children's drawings of bread making in order on a strip of paper and display on the wall.

ASSESSMENT
How closely does the child observe and explore the different items? Look out for signs that the older child is able to link the animal with its products.

If the child is able to put the different items in order (cow, milk, butter and so on) this will show her understanding of the processes you have talked about.

EARLY LEARNING GOALS
Knowledge and Understanding of the World:
Find out about, and identify, some features of living things, objects and events they observe.
Observe, find out about and identify features in the place they live and the natural world.
Ask questions about why things happen and how things work.
Look closely at similarities, differences, patterns and change.
Communication, Language and Literacy:
Enjoy listening to and using spoken and written language, and readily turn to it in their play and learning.
Sustain attentive listening, responding to what they have heard by relevant comments, questions or actions.
Extend their vocabulary.
Creative Development:
Respond in a variety of ways to what they see, hear, smell, touch and feel.

A C T I V I T Y - *Being helpful*

ABOUT THE ACTIVITY
Farmer Duck contains some strong moral messages about how to behave. The events of the story make a good starting point for talking about helpfulness and related behaviours such as being lazy or how you act when you are concerned about somebody else.

GROUP
Up to four children at a time.

WHAT YOU WILL NEED
Farmer Duck
Clip-board and marker pen
Paper for making a book
Photographs or drawings of each child

WHAT TO DO
Once you have read *Farmer Duck* a few times, look specifically at the moral message of the story. Talk about how the duck felt when he was left to do all the work, and how much happier he felt when all the other animals shared the work. What do the children think about the lazy farmer? Ask older ones what they would have done if they had been one of the animals on the farm.

Making a helpful book: Talk about the different ways in which each child in the group is helpful - to parents, to grandparents, to brothers and sisters, friends and neighbours. Encourage each child to come up with an example. If they cannot think of anything, help them by referring to a pre-school task - collecting the paintings to be handed out at home time or setting out the cups for snack time. Talk about how they feel when they have been helpful and how the person they have helped feels.

Make a note of each child's helpful action, using your clip-board and marker pen. Ask children to bring in photographs from home or do drawings of themselves. Older ones can also do portraits of each other. Write up each child's action using the same wording each time: *Alice is very helpful. She helps her daddy weed the garden / Ashram is very helpful. He helps his big sister walk the dog.*

Fold sheets of sugar paper in half and stick the words and pictures onto the pages so that each child has a page to herself. Attach the pages to make a book (see 'Making a book', page 11). Give the book a title, such as 'Our helpful book'. Read through the pages with the children from time to time. Older children can look at the book themselves. The repeated wording on each page will help those who are starting to read independently.

A weekly helpful task: Encourage the children to concentrate on being helpful in their day-to-day lives by thinking of one or two helpful acts to focus on each week. What you choose will depend on the routines in your setting. You may have a particular problem you want to focus on, such as a garden toy that a number of children squabble over. Make the weekly helpful task sharing the toy and help the children to do this on a day-to-day basis. Encourage the children to decide what some of the tasks should be. Once you have decided, write them on a large piece of paper to pin on the wall and remind the children at the start of each session.

ASSESSMENT
Is the child able to contribute to the discussion by drawing on her experiences of helping others? How confidently does she express herself during the discussion? Once you have decided on the weekly helpful task, make a note of which children remember and attempt to carry it out.

EARLY LEARNING GOALS
Personal, Social and Emotional Development:
Work as part of a group or class, taking turns and sharing fairly, understanding that there needs to be agreed values and codes of behaviour for groups of people, including adults and children, to work together harmoniously.
Have a developing awareness of their own needs, views and feelings and be sensitive to the needs, views and feelings of others.
Form good relationships with adults and peers.
Communication, Language and Literacy:
Interact with others, negotiating plans and activities and taking turns in conversation.
Knowledge and Understanding of the World:
Find out about, and identify, some features of living things, objects and events they observe.

F I V E - M I N U T E   A C T I V I T I E S

OLD MACDONALD
Sing 'Old Macdonald had a farm', using the animals in the *Farmer Duck* story. You could change the name 'Old Macdonald' to 'Farmer Duck'.

SORTING ANIMAL ITEMS
Gather model animals and various linked items:
- a model sheep, a ball of wool, knitting needles, woolly clothes, a lamb
- a model hen, an eggshell, a model chick, an egg box, an egg cup
- a model cow, a milk carton, a yoghurt carton, a tub of butter, a model calf
Set out the three animals, mix up the items and help the children to sort them into their three groups.

GUESS THE ANIMAL
Choose a farm animal and describe it to the children - colour, size, shape, what it produces and finally the sound it makes. Can the children guess which animal you are talking about? Vary your clues to suit the ages of the children in the group.

Planning chart

Activity	Themes	Page
Grandpa's Handkerchief		
Role play with handkerchiefs	Colour; Days of the week	25
Colour sorting with objects	Colour	26
Printing handkerchiefs	Colour; Pattern	27
Dear Zoo		
Animal flaps	Size; Shape	29
Pets	Animals; Pets; Pet care	30
The zoo	Animals	31
Mr Gumpy's Outing		
Making animal props	Animal features	34
Role play	Animal behaviour; Sequences; Cause and effect; Full/empty; Water	35
Sink and float	Sinking/floating; Water	36
The ending	Stories; Story endings	37
The Blue Balloon		
Exploring balloons	Size; Shape; Change; Air; Floating/sinking; Static electricity	39
Shapes, sizes and colours	Colour; Size; Shape	41
Sorting balloons	Colour; Size; Shape	42
Where will the balloon take you?	Journeys; Story endings	43
Washing line		
Exploring clothes	Clothes; Seasons; Weather	45
Matching animals and garments	Size; Shape	46
Washing line number sequence	Numbers from 1 to 5	47
Size and opposites	Size and dimension; Opposites	48
Painted collage	Colour; Pattern	50
The Very Hungry Caterpillar		
Making butterflies	Colour; Pattern; Butterflies	51
Life-cycle of a butterfly	Life-cycles	52
Menus for a hungry caterpillar	Food; Days of the week	53
Making a number sequence	Numbers 1 to 10	54

Activity	Themes	Page
Rosie's Walk		
Our walk	Position words; Orienteering	55
A map of Rosie's farmyard	Position words	56
Looking at trees	Trees and leaves; Pattern	57
Ten, Nine, Eight		
Body counting	Numbers from 1 to 10; The body	60
Toys	Toys and toys from the past	61
Night and day	Night and day	62
The Nursery Collection		
Environmental qualities	Opposites/contrasts	64
Exploring the environment	Environmental qualities; Texture; Weight; Size and dimension; Sound	65
Movement opposites	Action and behaviour opposites; Position opposites; Position words	67
Dear Daddy		
Reading *Dear Daddy*	Story structure; The passage of time; Seasons; Weather; Letter writing; Family life	69
Writing letters	Letter writing - addresses, posting letters	70
Exploring vehicles	Vehicles (and how they move)	71
Weather charts	Weather; Seasons	73
Who's Who in Our Street?		
A weekly diary	Days of the week; Sequencing	75
Making a roster	Helpful tasks; Days of the week	76
Rooms in a house	Houses/homes	77
All kinds of houses	Houses/homes; Buildings	79
Farmer Duck		
Farmyard patchwork	Farm animals; Farms	81
Farmyard lotto	Farm animals	82
Farm produce	Farms; Farm animals and produce	83
Being helpful	Helping others	85

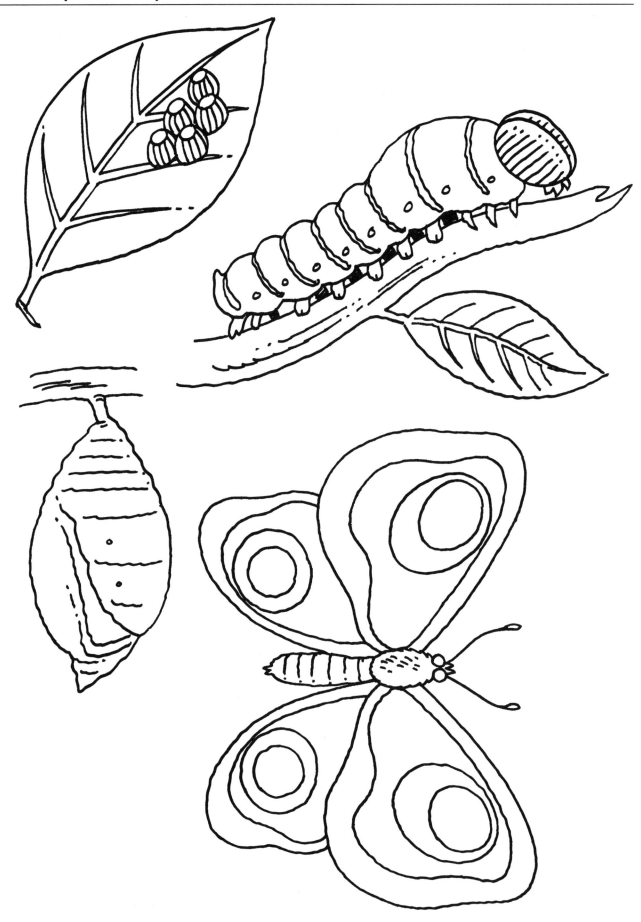